Following the

Following the Celtic Way

A new assessment of Celtic Christianity

Ian Bradley

DARTON·LONGMAN + TODD

First published in 2018 by
Darton, Longman and Todd Ltd
1 Spencer Court
140 – 142 Wandsworth High Street
London SW18 4JJ

ISBN: 978-0-232-53341-5

A catalogue record for this book is available from the British Library.

Phototypeset by Kerrypress, St Albans, Herts, AL3 8JL
Printed and bound in Great Britain by Bell & Bain, Glasgow

Contents

Preface   vii

Part 1 Clearing the Way

1   The modern revival of Celtic Christianity and its
continuing appeal   3

2   Defining Celtic Christianity   17

3   The sources   25

Part 2 Exploring the Way

4   Marks of the church and expressions of faith   43

5   Attributes of God   67

6   Appropriate human responses   95

7   Ways to follow   119

8   Some missing Ps – what we don't find in
Celtic Christianity   135

Part 3 Following the Way today

9   Following the Celtic Way today   141

Bibliography   159

Preface

The Celtic Way was first published 25 years ago in 1993. It has never been out of print and has been translated into Dutch and German. A second edition appeared in 2003 with a new preface reflecting on some of the changes and developments that had taken place in the Celtic Christian scene over the decade since its first publication, but otherwise its text has remained unchanged throughout this long period.

This anniversary seems an appropriate occasion for a completely new book which revisits the topic of Celtic Christianity in the light of the considerable research and rethinking that has taken place over the last 25 years. It will probably be my last word on the subject, at least in book form. I am now not too far off the three score years and ten which the Psalmist sees as the normal span of human life and even if my earthly pilgrimage continues for another decade or more I doubt that I will have anything very much more to say on this topic.

In many ways it would have been tempting to leave the original *Celtic Way* as it stands, as I did for the new 2003 edition. I have been immensely moved by the many letters I have received over the years from people telling me that reading it has changed and indeed in some cases saved their faith, brought them back to Christianity despite having profound difficulties with the church, and given them new direction and hope. However, research by myself and others has made me realise that the original book was coloured too much by the naive zeal of the new convert and was overly romantic and simplistic in some of what it said both about particular themes and also about the uniqueness and particularity of Celtic Christianity. I have also become more sceptical and cautious about the use of this phrase and the concept that it denotes.

My own developing thoughts around the whole area of what, for better or worse, is probably going to go on being referred to and thought of as Celtic Christianity, can be traced through six books that I have written since *The Celtic Way*. The first, *Columba:*

Pilgrim and Penitent (Wild Goose Publications, 1996), which was commissioned by the Iona Community, reflected on the life and legacy of the Irish monk and saint associated with Iona who has for me consistently been the most flesh-and-blood, embodied and appealing figure among the pantheon of saints from the 'golden age' of Celtic Christianity. It introduced several of the themes beginning with the letter 'P' which I reiterate and expand in the present volume. *Celtic Christianity – Making Myths and Dreaming Dreams* (Edinburgh University Press, 1999) has been my most academic and deconstructionist work in this area. Written partly under the influence of scholarly critics of the romanticism of *The Celtic Way*, it charted the way in which the concept of Celtic Christianity has essentially been an invented and re-invented construct carrying the dreams and myths of successive generations looking longingly back to a pure and primitive golden age into which Christians have projected their own dreams and their frustrations about what they have felt lacking in the church of their own times.

Colonies of Heaven (Darton, Longman and Todd, 2000), published in North America under the title *Celtic Christian Communities Live the Tradition*, sought to strip away the accretions and listen to the authentic voice of the early indigenous Christian communities of the British Isles in so far as we can still hear it. It explored and identified six broad themes – the monastic nature of the church; blessing and cursing; penance and pastoral care; worship, the communion of saints; and pilgrimage. Several of these themes are picked up again in the present volume, although the reader is directed back to that earlier book for more substantial treatment of them. In *Believing in Britain: The Spiritual Identity of 'Britishness'*, first published in hardback by I.B. Tauris in 2007 and then in paperback by Lion Books in 2008, I explored the Celtic, and more specifically the Welsh and Irish, contribution to British identity arguing that 'historically speaking, British identity is Celtic before it is anything else'. The theme of pilgrimage, which I have increasingly come to feel is both the most dominant and the most relevant of all aspects of the faith of our Celtic Christian ancestors, was further explored in *Pilgrimage: A Spiritual and Cultural Journey* (Lion, 2009) which has been translated into Dutch, Norwegian, Arabic and Japanese. Most recently, *Argyll: The Making of a Spiritual Landscape* (St Andrew Press, 2015) presents a detailed picture of the spiritual landscape of a region exhibiting in particularly dramatic form the characteristics generally associated with Celtic Christianity and which I encapsulated as combining evangelical simplicity and liberal mysticism.

So, what follows can be taken at one level as the final fruit of the nearly three decades that I have now spent researching, lecturing, teaching, preaching, writing, broadcasting and reflecting on this subject. To some extent, *Following The Celtic Way* synthesizes, embraces and incorporates what I have discovered and expressed in the six books mentioned above and also what I have learned from the many other books published over the last quarter century. In some respects, it returns to and reiterates some of the central themes which I first identified and explored at the start of my journey of discovery into this fascinating, elusive and strangely appealing period of our Christian past and which I expressed in *The Celtic Way*. They include presence, protection, praise and, above all, pilgrimage. But there are other elements that I highlighted in that first book which I now feel need to be substantially modified if not discarded. I am, for example, no longer inclined to view Celtic Christianity as either feminine – or eco-friendly, light on sin and judgement or particularly affirmative of the natural world and the intrinsic goodness of humanity. I am much more conscious of the orthodoxy of the faith of the early Irish monks, their sense of human sinfulness and the importance of penitence and their belief in the awesome power as well as the presence of God. I realise that, like others who wrote in those early heady days of the modern Celtic Christian revival, I was somewhat careless in conflating ancient and relatively modern sources and seeing them all as representing a single continuing entity. I was also too ready to project my own dreams and prejudices into the mists of the far-distant past.

In researching this book, I have returned to the original sources which survive from the indigenous Christian communities of Ireland, Wales, Scotland and the northern and western fringes of England between the fifth and eleventh centuries. They include saints' lives, letters, prayers, poems, sermons, penitentials and rules, almost all of which were written in monasteries and belong to a monastic context. I have read them more closely and carefully than I did when writing *The Celtic Way* and the effect that they have had on me has been very different from that produced by more cursory encounters with them 25 years ago. I have found my own very liberal Christian faith seriously challenged rather than reinforced and I have been made much more conscious of my own sin and frailty and of the themes of judgement and accountability. This has been a much harder and more disturbing journey than the one which originally took me on to the Celtic way. Maybe that is because I am older than when I first embarked on it but I think it is also because I have let the voices of the Celtic saints, their followers and chroniclers, speak to me more clearly and listened to them with less of a preconceived agenda about what I was hoping to hear from them. If they have not quite turned this unrepentant old liberal into a conservative evangelical, they have certainly forced me think much more seriously about subjects which are not naturally congenial to me.

This book is presented in three parts. The first, Clearing the Way, surveys the present revival of interest in Celtic Christianity and what lies behind it, seeks to define this beguiling but elusive entity and discusses the main sources for gaining information and understanding of the faith and practice of Celtic-speaking Christians living in the British Isles between the fifth and eleventh centuries. The second part, Exploring the Way, which can be taken as the heart of the book, identifies and examines 21 key beliefs and practices of Celtic Christianity, grouped under the headings of Marks of the church and expressions of faith; Attributes of God; Appropriate human responses; and Ways to follow. These are encapsulated in words or phrases all beginning with the letter P. I began this particular alliterative obsession in my book on Columba where I identified nine key themes in the Columban church – a devotional base built on prayer, psalms and poetry; a theology of praise, protection and presence and an ecclesiology (not, as I pointed out, a word that Columba and his followers would ever have dreamed of using) of penitence, provisionality and pilgrimage. These nine Ps continue to feature prominently in the present book with another twelve added. I am not quite sure why I am so fixated on this alliterative approach or on this particular letter of the alphabet. I can only crave my readers' indulgence for this slightly strange obsession and hope that they will regard it with the same friendly amusement as the group to whom I lectured on this subject in Iona Abbey in May 2017 and from whom at the end of the week I received a bag of Birds Eye frozen peas! There is also a brief chapter at the end of this middle part enumerating some of the 'P' words which are not found in Celtic Christianity. The third part of the book offers a concluding chapter suggesting some pointers for those wishing to follow the Celtic way today.

25 years on from *The Celtic Way*, this new book offers a more sober and measured appreciation of a significant tradition, perhaps one less exceptional or unique than I once thought, but nonetheless distinctive and important. It is still an appreciation nonetheless and one which I hope will help those who read it on their own spiritual journeys and deepen and enliven their faith. I hope that it is scholarly and accurate in what it says but it is also intended to be accessible, engaging and to appeal at the spiritual level as much as the historical. I hope it will encourage its readers to follow the Celtic way, which for all its twists and turns, its paradoxes, ambiguities and frustrations, its difficulties and challenges, I continue to believe is one which can bring us closer to Christ, his teachings and purposes for us and the coming of his kingdom.

Part 1

Clearing the Way

1

The modern revival of Celtic Christianity and its continuing appeal

The Celtic Way first appeared at the height of the modern revival of interest in and enthusiasm for Celtic Christianity. The origins of this revival can perhaps be traced back to the 1960s when a number of paperback anthologies of prayers started appearing culled largely from the *Carmina Gadelica*, the collection of Gaelic prayers, blessings and incantations collected in the late nineteenth century by Alexander Carmichael. There were other significant stirrings in the late 1960s and early 1970s. The American monk and spiritual writer, Thomas Merton, noted in his journal: 'I am reading about Celtic monasticism, the hermits, the lyric poets, the pilgrims, the sea travellers, etc. A whole new world that has waited until now to open up for me' (Sellner 1993:9). Sadly he was to die in 1968 before he could explore it further. The distinguished Scottish theologian John Macquarrie in his *Paths in Spirituality*, a book written in 1972 when he was Lady Margaret Professor of Divinity in the University of Oxford, presented Celtic Christian spirituality as a counter model to the dominant culture of secular materialism in modern western society.

It was in the 1990s that interest in Celtic Christianity, understood primarily in terms of the indigenous Christian faith of the British Isles in the so-called dark ages between the fifth and tenth centuries but also embracing much later material in Irish, Scots Gaelic and Welsh collected by the likes of Carmichael, really took off at a popular level. A clutch of books which appeared through the decade under the imprint of well-established Christian publishers portrayed Celtic Christianity as embracing certain distinctive themes with a strong contemporary relevance. Among the first in the field was Robert Van de Weyer's *Celtic Fire* (1990) which posited three main influences on Celtic Christianity: ancient Druid religion, the Egyptian Desert Fathers, and the 'great British heretic, Pelagius'. It was closely followed by Esther de Waal's *A World Made Whole – The Rediscovery of the Celtic Tradition* (1991). My own *The Celtic Way* appeared in 1993, as did one of the first North American contributions to the current wave of interest, Edward Sellner's *Wisdom of the Celtic Saints*. They were followed by a trinity of similar volumes in 1995, Michael Mitton's *Restoring the Woven Cord: Strands of Celtic Christianity for the Church Today*, Ray Simpson's *Exploring Celtic Spirituality: Historic Roots For Our Future* and Philip Sheldrake's *Living Between Worlds: Place and Journey in Celtic Spirituality*. Common to all these books which appeared in the early 1990s was a conviction that Celtic Christianity was a distinct movement and entity which embraced a gentle spirituality and an affirmative view of human nature. Among the books published in 1997 was *Listening for the Heartbeat of God: A Celtic Spirituality* by Philip Newell, a popular and influential Presbyterian retreat director and author who has remained one of the prime exponents of this approach, positing a distinctive Celtic Christianity strongly influenced by St John's Gospel and deeply creation-centred in its approach.

In the early days of the revival, Celtic Christianity tended to find its greatest enthusiasts among those in the more liberal and catholic wings of the church. Liberals like me were attracted by what seemed a less hierarchical, dogmatic and sin-centred inculturation of Christianity where there was more emphasis on free spirits, blessing and affirmation as against judgement and condemnation. It seemed to offer a faith that was holistic, affirmative of the natural world and less anthropocentric than many other forms of Christianity. Catholics were attracted by its spirituality and mysticism, themes emphasized by Noel O'Donoghue in his books, *The Mountain Behind the Mountain: Aspects of the Celtic Tradition* (1993) and *The Angels Keep Their Ancient Places: Reflections on Celtic Spirituality* (2001). Written in a mystical stream of consciousness style, and in many ways spiritual autobiographies, his books could be taken as pleas for the preservation of mystery at a time when Celtic Christianity was becoming increasingly appealing as a subject for academic study and postgraduate theses. Another prime exemplar of this mystical Catholic approach in the 1990s was John O'Donohue, an Irish priest, philosopher and poet, whose *Anam Cara: A Book of Celtic Wisdom*, first published in 1998 as 'a guide through the spiritual landscape of the Irish imagination' became an international bestseller. In the United States, the Catholic contribution to the current Celtic Christian revival has been strong, epitomised by Edward Sellner and by Timothy Joyce, a Benedictine monk of Irish descent, in his book *Celtic Christianity: A Sacred Tradition, a Vision of Hope* (1998).

With some exceptions, notably Ray Simpson and Michael Mitton, conservative evangelical Christians tended to shun the revival in its early days. This was partly because of their feeling that Celtic Christianity was dangerously New Age and neo-pagan. It was certainly the case that some of the earliest books to appear in the current revival, notably Shirley Toulson's *The Celtic Alternative: A Reminder of the Christianity We Lost* (1987), Michael Howard's *Angels and Goddesses* (1994), Caitlin Matthews' *The Celtic Tradition* (1995) and Chalwyn James' *An Age of Saints: Its Relevance For Us Today* (1996) were written from a syncretistic rather than a distinctly Christian perspective, appeared under the imprint of 'New Age' publishers and played up the closeness of Celtic paganism and Celtic Christianity. This broad syncretistic agenda is still present, expressed in an increasing tendency to talk of Celtic spirituality rather than Celtic Christianity and in a penchant on the part of booksellers to shelve books on the subject in the 'Body, Mind and Spirit' sections of their shops rather than under 'Christianity' or even 'religion'.

One of the more interesting developments through the 1990s was the shift and broadening of the appeal of Celtic Christianity from those of 'New Age', liberal and Catholic persuasions to embrace evangelicals and charismatics. Charismatics rightly came to see much that they could affirm in a spirituality which emphasized miracles, prophecy, signs and wonders, angelic and diabolical presences. It was notable that both Simpson and Mitton came from a charismatic evangelical Anglican tradition. Also important to evangelicals was a sense that Celtic Christianity offered a particular approach to mission relevant in the modern age. This was the thesis of John Finney, officer for the Decade of Evangelism in the Church of England for much of the 1990s, in his book *Recovering the Past: Celtic and Roman mission* (1996) which like many others contrasted a Celtic and a Roman approach, the former culture-friendly and the latter institutional, hierarchical and top-down. Finney suggested that the Celtic model of mission, which he identified as prioritizing spirituality over doctrine and emphasizing community rather than hard-selling the Gospel, was more effective for reaching a society like ours that is predominantly non-Christian in its make-up. A similar approach was taken by the American writer George Hunter III in his *The Celtic Way of Evangelism: How Christianity Can Reach the West Again* (2000). Through the 2000s a number of books appeared from evangelical authors, especially in the United States, warmly embracing Celtic Christianity.

Alongside this growing band of enthusiasts from across the theological and denominational spectrum, there were also a number of sceptics and scoffers. I still cherish a postcard I received from the then editor of the *Church Times* in 1994 following an enthusiastic piece I had written. It simply said: 'You don't altogether overcome my sense that Celtic spirituality belongs in Pseuds' Corner'. The most sustained critique of the whole Celtic Christian revival came from Donald Meek, a distinguished Celtic scholar at Aberdeen and Edinburgh universities. His first sally, in a review article in the *Scottish Bulletin of Evangelical Theology* in 1991, made a point to which he would come back again and again: 'There is a very real danger that pilgrims on this re-discovered Celtic way will see in 'Celtic Christianity' a mirror image of their own desires for a meaningful encounter with "spirituality", with "wholeness", with "being"' (Meek 1991:14). His critique reached its fullest expression in his book: *The Quest for Celtic Christianity* (2000). Noting that '"Celtic Christianity" tends to flourish in proportion to its distance from the real Celtic sources', he re-stated his central thesis that 'at the heart of "Celtic Christianity", as popularly constructed, lies a highly creative approach to the reconstruction of the past' (Meek 2000:2). His book chronicled what he saw as 'the creation of a romantic spirituality' influenced by modern liberal theology and a desire to be closer to nature where generalization, wishful thinking and fundamentally poor scholarship had distorted an inculturation of Christianity which was, in reality, theologically conservative, highly Biblical and not in the least friendly towards paganism.

It was not just those of a conservative evangelical persuasion who expressed unease at the assertions being made by the modern enthusiasts for Celtic Christianity. The Roman Catholic scholar Gilbert Márkus was especially active in demolishing cherished shibboleths, arguing that there was nothing specifically Pelagian about early Irish Christianity and that Celtic saints did not have any particularly close relationship with the animal world. In an important book co-authored with the Celtic scholar Tom Clancy, he pointed out that 'the speakers of Celtic languages – British, Irish and Picts – had no more contact with each other than with the Anglo-Saxons or people from the continent, except by force of geography and they had no conception that they were related to each other, even distantly'. (Clancy & Márkus 1995:8). In an article published in 1997 provocatively entitled 'The End of Celtic Christianity', Márkus adduced evidence to suggest that far from being egalitarian, anti-Roman, feminine friendly and Pelagian, Celtic Christianity was, in fact, hierarchical, subordinate to and in close conformity with Rome, markedly chauvinistic and distinguished by an exceptionally strong attachment to the doctrine of the Fall and the reality of Hell. He concluded that the excessive romanticism of the modern revival would puncture the myth of Celtic Christianity for good: 'it doesn't actually preserve anything or introduce us to our Christian fathers and mothers, but is simply the last nail in the coffin of the Celtic Christian past' (Márkus 1997:54).

These and other assaults did not stop the Celtic Christian bandwagon from rolling on. They did, however, give some of us who were enthusiastic about this movement pause for reflection. The work of Meek and Márkus in particular led me to rethink my own position and tone down some of the wilder and more romantic claims I had made in *The Celtic Way*. It prompted me to ponder the way in which the insular Christianity of the British Isles from the fifth to the tenth centuries had so often been appealed to as a repository of all those values which people have found lacking in their own time. My *Celtic Christianity – Making Myths and Dreaming Dreams* (1997) traced seven revivals over the last 1300 years, including the present one, in which the whole concept of Celtic Christianity had effectively been invented and re-invented to suit the agenda of successive generations of Christians.

Another important corrective to inflated claims about the uniqueness of Celtic Christian spirituality was provided by two popular books by academics published in 1999 about Anglo-Saxon Christianity. Benedicta Ward's *High King of Heaven* and Paul Cavill's *Anglo-Saxon Christianity* clearly demonstrated that many of the characteristics generally taken to be distinctively Celtic, including monasticism and the eremitical life, love of the psalms and a sense of the closeness of the saints and heaven, were equally to be found in early English Christianity. Ward pointed out that the Anglo-Saxon crosses at Ruthwell and Bewcastle pre-date the earliest surviving Irish high crosses. Cavill suggested that early English spirituality was, in fact, more balanced and earthed than Celtic Christianity which he characterised as adopting a dualist approach which held the physical sphere to be evil and advocated a radical separation between secular and religious life. The overall message of these and other more recent scholarly studies has been that the Christian life of the British Isles in the early mediaeval period was an amalgam of several different influences and cannot be sharply divided into competing Celtic, Roman and Anglo-Saxon factions or compartments. They have also demonstrated that the early English were every bit as spiritual as their Irish, Scottish and Welsh neighbours.

Perhaps partly in response to these challenges, there has been a marked diminution in the number of books coming out on the subject of Celtic Christianity over the last two decades, compared with the flood in the 1990s. However, the stream has by no means dried up. As well as regular reprints of books like *The Celtic Way*, there has been a steady trickle of new studies, notably of individual Celtic saints, places and other more specialised themes. There have also been more recent general books, still very much in the spirit of those from the early heady days of the current revival. Philip Newell, in particular, continues to argue in books such as *Christ of the Celts: The Healing of Creation* (2008) that Celtic Christianity did have a distinctively holistic, affirming creation-centred spirituality in contrast to later Augustine-dominated western Christianity. The strong continuing interest in this area in the United States is testified to in such recent books as Kenneth McIntosh's *Water from an Ancient Well: Celtic Spirituality for Modern* Life (2011). Among the early enthusiasts, Ray Simpson continues to be the most prolific, with numerous prayer anthologies, books about specific themes such as *Aidan of Lindisfarne*, a novel about Aidan and, most recently, *New Celtic Monasticism for everyday people* (2014), one of a number of studies spawned by the strong contemporary interest in what is called new monasticism and the growth of intentional communities based, among other models, on the Irish monasteries.

Among Donald Meek's more telling observations about the modern revival, which he characterised as 'the new Celtic religious movement', is that it has been a very bookish affair, comfortable and undemanding in its approach, with an unscholarly and erroneous emphasis on such themes as closeness to nature, gentleness and primitive simplicity at the expense of the more brutal, austere and severe elements undoubtedly present in the early Christianity of the British Isles. As he points out, 'Few of the movement's advocates have yet taken to living on Rockall or the Old Man of Hoy, although such eremetic sites offer stacks of potential, in keeping with the aspirations of several Celtic saints' (Meek 1992:9). It is true that the modern enthusiasts for Celtic Christianity have not sought to follow the ascetic ways of the Irish monks and subject themselves to standing for hours up to their waists in cold water, fasting for days on end and genuflecting all night. Rather we have sat in the comfort of our studies tapping away on computers to produce appealing and comforting volumes on holistic spirituality. But although it is true to say that one of the most conspicuous features of the current revival has been a plethora of attractive paperback anthologies of prayers and spiritual manuals, it has also had other more practical and physical manifestations.

Worship is one area of contemporary church life and witness which has been significantly affected by the modern Celtic Christian revival. It has directly spawned a number of Celtic praise bands, notably Iona which was started by David Fitzgerald and Dave Bainbridge in 1989 and Sammy Horner's Celtic Praise, as well as a huge number of CDs of Celtic style or inspired Christian music. Many churches have put on Celtic services – this can involve anything from featuring a harp or clarsach, using the prayers of David Adam or those from *Carmina Gadelica* to singing the songs of John Bell and the Wild Goose Group, the worship group of the Iona Community which has itself taken a slightly detached position with regard to the revival. A vast number of self-styled Celtic liturgies and worship books have been published. Among the most significant from the early years of the modern revival are *Celtic Daily Prayer, a Northumbrian Office* published by the Northumbria Community, *Each Day & Each Night: A Weekly Cycle of Prayers from Iona in the Celtic Tradition* by Philip Newell (both 1994) and *Celtic Worship Through the Year* and *Celtic Daily Light: A Spiritual Journey Through the Year*, both compiled by Ray Simpson and published in 1997. In 2003 Ray Simpson brought out *The Celtic Prayer Book*, a four-volume blockbuster. How Celtic these actually are is debatable – their modern prayers, written in English, are often simple and poetic and sometimes themed around Celtic saints but have a much broader scope. Other liturgies recycle material from the *Carmina Gadelica*. The Church of Scotland's 1994 *Book of Common Order* included for the first time consciously 'Celtic' orders for both morning and evening services modelled partly on the rhythmic, repetitive style found in some early Irish prayers but more obviously drawing from much later material. However authentic or not it may actually be, Celtic worship has taken its place alongside prayers and chants from Taizé as one of the main growth areas in contemporary liturgy, providing something simple, direct, meditative, rhythmic and poetic which undoubtedly has an appeal across denominations and theological traditions.

Another area where the revival of interest in Celtic Christianity has had a direct impact on the church is in the growth of dispersed intentional communities. The two most significant religious movements to emerge from the current revival both take their inspiration from the island of Lindisfarne, or Holy Island, associated with Aidan and Cuthbert, and the site of the Northumbrian monastery which was in reality as much Anglo-Saxon as Celtic. The Northumbria community was established in 1992 when a small group of charismatic Christians from different denominations moved into a large house in north Northumberland, which stands near a cave where Cuthbert's body is said to have been carried by monks from Lindisfarne fleeing from Viking invaders. They included a Baptist minister, an Anglican priest, and a lay Roman Catholic who had drawn inspiration from the rhythm of daily prayer they experienced on Lindisfarne while living there in the late 1970s. What brought them together was a conviction 'of the importance of the Celtic brand of Christianity, its emphasis on monastery and mission, the fire of continual devotion, and obedience to the initiatives of the Spirit'. (Raine & Skinner 1994: 443). The community has members dispersed throughout the country who follow a way of living that emphasizes availability and vulnerability. There is a strong focus on mission, developing techniques of spiritual warfare associated with the Celtic saints, music and liturgy.

The Community of Aidan and Hilda is similarly rooted in the charismatic renewal movement. It was launched in 1994 at an Anglican renewal conference by a group which included Michael

Mitton and Ray Simpson. It draws direct inspiration from the lives of Northumbrian saints and seeks the revival of their particular brand of Christian practice and witness today. The community is specifically committed 'to restore the memory, landmarks, witness and experience of the Celtic church in ways that relate to God's purposes today, and to research the history, beliefs, lifestyle, evangelism and relationships to cultural patterns of the Celtic church and how they apply to the renewal of today's church and society'(Simpson 1995:11). Those seeking to join the Community are first allocated a soul friend who guides them in 'the first voyage of the coracle' which leads to becoming a member and subscribing to a rule of life which involves a commitment to prayer, study, care for creation, mission and wholeness and also to 'becoming familiar with such saints as Aidan, Brigid, Columba, David, Illtyd, Ninian, Oswald and Patrick. We·remember their feast days and consider them as companions on our journey of faith'. Members are spread across the world, with significant chapters in North America, Australia and Norway.

Both these communities are part of a wider movement known as the new monasticism which is leading many Christians to explore ways of living more intentional lives in some kind of community with a shared rule of life and discipline of prayer. Celtic Christianity is only one influence behind this – there is also much interest in Benedictine monasticism – but there is no doubt that the monastic character of the early church in the British Isles, to some extent paralleled in the institution of the minster in the Anglo-Saxon church, is of great contemporary interest and is being seen as a model for churches today as the parish system which replaced it is collapsing.

Perhaps the most striking physical expression of the current revival of Celtic Christianity is the upsurge of interest and participation in pilgrimage. Celtic Christian sites like Iona, Lindisfarne, and places associated with Irish and Welsh saints, are attracting substantial and growing numbers of visitors, many of whom describe themselves as pilgrims. New pilgrim ways are being developed across the British Isles following in the footsteps of the Celtic saints and linking ancient ecclesiastical and monastic sites, one of the first being St Cuthbert's Way from Melrose to Lindisfarne which opened in 1996. The current revival of pilgrimage and its ramifications will be discussed more fully in the closing chapter of this book.

There has been little attempt to create a new denomination based on the supposed distinctive tenets of Celtic Christianity although there is a tiny Celtic Orthodox Church which has bases in Brittany, England and Wales and links with the Syrian Orthodox Church. In the United States there are also a small number of self-styled Celtic churches, some of which come under the umbrella of the Celtic Christian Communion. There are several virtual Celtic communities and monasteries on the internet but they are fewer in number now than in the heyday of the current revival in the 1990s.

Overall, enthusiasm for Celtic Christianity is not what it was when *The Celtic Way* first came out in the early 1990s. Yet it has by no means disappeared. Seminars, study days and retreats on the subject still attract a good number of participants. I am told that the weeks which I lead on Celtic Christianity in Iona Abbey sell out more quickly than any of the other themed programme weeks run by the Iona Community. Even though it may have peaked, the current revival still has some way to go before it runs out of steam.

What are the reasons for the continuing contemporary interest in Celtic Christianity? I can think of several, closely interlinked, and there may well be more. The first is the phenomenon of the decline of religion and rise of spirituality which has been noted by many commentators as a striking feature of our age. In this context religion is associated with dogma, creeds, churchgoing, institutions, authorities and hierarchies. Spirituality, by contrast, embraces personal experience and practice, engaged emotion and heightened consciousness and awareness. This trend has been most clearly identified and highlighted, at least in the British context, in the seminal study, *The Spiritual Revolution: Why Religion is Giving Way to Spirituality*, by Paul Heelas and Linda Woodhead of the University of Lancaster, published in 2004. It has been further chronicled and examined in other more recent studies and could be said in many ways to have replaced the secularization thesis as a way of summarizing and providing an overview of what is happening to religious life and belief in the west, and particularly in Britain. Surveys continue to show steadily falling levels of church attendance and participation in formal religious observances and declining belief in traditional theism and religious doctrines, especially traditional Christian ones, while at the same time showing growing interest in the practice of mindfulness, meditation and other spiritual techniques.

Celtic Christianity appeals much more to people today as a spirituality than as a religion – indeed the terms Celtic Christianity and Celtic spirituality are used interchangeably and without much distinction. The first modern usage of the phrase 'Celtic spirituality' than I can find is in John Macquarrie's 1972 book *Paths in Spirituality*. There has been a long tradition, going back at least as far as nineteenth century romantics and enthusiasts like Ernest Rénan and Matthew Arnold, of seeing the Celts as a particularly spiritual people, somehow more mystical and in touch with their spiritual sides than the more prosaic, literal minded Anglo-Saxons. John Lorne Campbell, the twentieth century Scottish folklorist, saw the Gaelic mind as vertical – touching the other world of spiritual and psychic experience – in contrast to the modern European mind which he characterized as horizontal – broad but not deep. Other writers have reinforced this myth of the spiritual Gael. In the context of the modern 'spiritual revolution' Celtic Christianity appeals as being somehow more spiritual and less religious than other types of Christianity that have been more prevalent in the west. It appears to be less doctrine ridden, propositional and wordy and more engaged, experiential and emotional.

This appeal is enhanced by a second related contemporary trend which is a move away from the rational and towards the mystical. This has several manifestations. It can seem like a flight from reason into an escapist irrationality and mumbo-jumbo superstitiousness, as evidenced by the growing appeal of tarot cards, astrology and the para-normal. It is also evidenced in a more 'touchy-feely' attitude and approach, as shown in new ritualised responses to death and grieving and more public displays of emotion on both a communal and individual level. Celtic Christianity seems to offer much in the mystical line, with its saints performing miracles and prophesying, its highly developed angelology, poetic prayers and icon-like illuminated manuscripts and high standing crosses. At the same time, it is light on long sermons and treatises on systematic theology. It appears to express faith much more in terms of images than propositions. This enhances its appeal in an age where religion, reason and theology are losing ground to mystical experience. A third related factor also comes into play here which is a growing preference for the physical and experiential over the purely intellectual and cerebral.

Even if the current Celtic Christian revival has been a largely bookish affair, what its leading proponents have written about is not so much theological doctrines and creeds as engaged spirituality and physical practices, notably prayer and pilgrimage.

There has also undoubtedly been an ecological and environmental dimension to the appeal of Celtic Christianity. This was particularly evident in the early years of the current revival. Noting how it 'does seem to speak with uncanny relevance to many of the concerns of our present age' I wrote in the preface to *The Celtic Way*, 'it was environment-friendly, embracing positive attitudes to nature and constantly celebrating the goodness of God's creation' (Bradley 1993: vii-viii). Like others, I was attracted to all those stories which at face value seem to show that the Celtic saints and monks were especially close to animals and birds and to the poems and prayers which ostensibly express a deep affinity and respect for the natural world. Alas, Celtic scholars have suggested that these texts are not all that they seem and seriously called into question the eco- friendly green credentials of Celtic Christianity. I found myself compelled to retract some of the earlier statements that I had made on this subject in *The Celtic Way*. I did so in an article entitled 'How green was Celtic Christianity?' published in the journal *Ecotheology* in 1998. Although it gives me no pleasure at all to do so, on the basis of my re-reading of many of the primary sources and also the commentaries on them by scholars, I have also felt the need to retract my early endorsement of the apparently feminine-friendly character of Celtic Christianity. This perceived aspect has been another undoubted reason for its appeal. I fear that the more I read and reflect on the monastic texts from Ireland, Scotland and Wales in the early mediaeval period, the more convinced I am that for the Celtic monks at least, Christian faith was conceived and expressed in very masculine if not even macho terms. Indeed, I find myself in agreement with the early mediaeval historian, Caitlin Corning, in her assessment that 'the Irish and British were no more pro-women, pro-environment or even spiritual than the rest of the Church' (Corning 2006:1).

If Celtic Christianity appeals today partly because of its perceived spiritual, green and feminist credentials, however erroneous they may be, there is also a whole cluster of reasons for its contemporary popularity bound up with the lure of the distant and primal past, tradition, roots and identity. As we know all too well, there is a widespread sense of alienation and disconnection in contemporary society. Many people are searching for roots and a sense of belonging. Celtic Christianity takes us back deep into our own past – and this seems to be true not just for those living in the British Isles but for its many enthusiasts in Continental Europe and North America. It has the appeal of the primitive and primal which has also fuelled considerable recent interest in Australian aboriginal and native American spirituality. It also has the appeal of the liminal, the marginal and the exotic in our midst, qualities which have been emphasized in previous Celtic Christian revivals. We do not need to go to the other side of the world to find a culture and spirituality which is different and exotic. It is there on our doorstep, in some of the most beautiful parts of the British Isles. It lends itself to being explored and presented in television programmes such as the immensely popular and much-repeated series presented by the archaeologist Neil Oliver entitled *The Sacred Wonders of Britain*.

In part, of course, the appeal of Celtic Christianity is just one aspect of a much broader modern appreciation of all things Celtic which has made traditional Welsh and Scottish music and Irish *Riverdance* so popular. Again, there are resonances here with roots, tribalism and national identity. There is also a more specific explanation for its particular lure. It seems to offer a return to a purer, simpler faith. This has been a recurrent theme across the various Celtic Christian revivals which have occurred over the last thousand years and more. As I observe in my *Celtic Christianity: Making Myths and Chasing Dreams*, which traces the course of six such revivals including the current one, 'a persistent vein of nostalgia has allowed those Christians who lived in Celtic-speaking regions in the sixth and seventh centuries, about whose faith and work we know next to nothing first hand, to become paragons of a pure and primitive faith' (Bradley 1999: ix). The beauty of Celtic Christianity for many of its modern devotees is precisely that it is so misty and shadowy, so short on hard facts and reliable sources, so surrounded by romantic myths and so susceptible to being re-invented and re-imagined. It is time to strip away these romantic accretions and inventions and try to pin down and define Celtic Christianity in terms of what it actually was and what we are left with, even if this means losing something of its mystery and spiritual aura. The next chapter seeks to begin this process of clearing the Celtic way.

2
Defining Celtic Christianity

How do we define Celtic Christianity? In the context of the modern revival, and indeed of earlier ones, it is tempting to suggest that it is not an actual phenomenon defined in historical and geographical terms, but rather an artificial construct created out of wishful thinking, romantic nostalgia and the projection of all kinds of dreams about what should and might be. I remember asking a group of students half way through an MA course on Celtic Christianity what they understood by the phrase. Their definitions included 'an intense sense of presence and place', 'an intimate liaison between humanity and the totality of creation', 'a poetic rather than a rational approach to faith', 'an indigenous Trinitarian form of Christianity designed for free spirits', 'wholeness and mystery', 'a loving God revealed through his creation' and 'a non-hierarchical church specially rooted in place and culture'. When I asked them later what they found most lacking in their own churches and in modern forms of Christian worship and doctrine, I received remarkably similar answers.

Ours is not the first generation to project back our dreams and desires for a purer, more primitive church and creed onto the Celts. The fact is that 'Celtic' has long been a term attracting all sorts of definitions and with a huge capacity to be the vessel through which we can project our dreams. As the scholar of languages and creator of *The Hobbit*, J.R.R. Tolkien, observed more than fifty years ago: 'The term "Celtic" is a magic bag into which anything may be put, and out of which almost anything may come…Anything is possible in the fabulous Celtic twilight which is not so much a twilight of the gods as of reason.'

So are we simply dealing with a construct of our imaginations and dreamings? We need to begin with the word Celtic itself. It derives from the word *Keltoi* which was used by the ancient Greeks to describe those living in central and western Europe north of the Alps and beyond the Mediterranean world and therefore, by implication, barbarians beyond the pale of civilization. The Greek historian Hecataeus of Miletus was possibly the first to use the word around 500 BC to describe the inhabitants of modern-day France, Spain, Central Europe, Austria, Switzerland, the Balkans and Turkey. *Keltoi* seems to have been primarily a geographical rather than an ethnic description although it conveyed the idea of a warrior people who were non-urban, nomadic, bellicose and somewhat exotic. The Roman term *Galli* had somewhat similar applications and connotations. Galatia, the area in modern Turkey also known as Anatolia and Asia Minor, visited and evangelized by Paul in the mid-first century AD, seems to take its name from a similar root, leading some scholars to speculate that it may have been the original homeland of the Celts. The word 'Celtic' largely disappeared from use through the Middle Ages and was only recovered in the aftermath of the Renaissance and the Reformation and then more widely in the eighteenth century, when it came specifically to be applied to a group of languages spoken in the British Isles.

These origins are important because they remind us that 'Celtic' is a term imposed from outside. Patrick, Columba, David and their contemporaries would have had no sense themselves of being 'Celts' – it was not a term that they would have used or that would have meant anything to them. It was essentially a somewhat pejorative label imposed from outside. Much of the construction of the idea and the components of 'Celtic Christianity' has similarly come from outsiders, most of them English or North American.

There is considerable debate among archaeologists and historians as to who the Celts were, if indeed they actually existed as a distinctive ethnic or linguistic grouping. Some maintain that we can talk about a Celtic people or Celtic tribes who originated in the area of the Black Sea or the Caucuses and gradually moved westwards across Europe in the millennium or so before the birth of Jesus. Miranda Green asserts that by the time of Jesus' birth, the Celtic world stretched from Galatia in the East to Ireland in the West. She sees its culture as being distinguished by the adoption of iron as a commonly used material and points out that 'Celtic culture *per se* is generally considered to have come to an end around the end of the first century BC, when most of temperate Europe was subjected to the domination of the Roman world' (Green 1996:6). Other scholars maintain that there was no real shared Celtic heritage, identity or culture across Europe. It is true that 'Celtic' art, markedly different from Greek or Roman art and characterized by its use of scrolls and interleaved spirals and lines, often with animals and birds hidden among them, is found across much of Iron Age Europe from the Black Sea to Ireland. Notable early examples of such artwork found in excavations in Hallstat in Austria and La Tène in Switzerland, appear to date from the eighth and fifth centuries BC respectively. This, however, is a categorization and classification by relatively modern art historians, many of whom would argue that there was never a single homogeneous race with shared cultural artefacts even if there do seem to have been similarities in what was produced across Europe.

While 'Celtic' has been defined by some scholars both in terms of ethnicity and art, the most prevalent and generally accepted definition has been in terms of language. Specifically, the word has been applied to the languages spoken by the native inhabitants of the British Isles and especially to those living in its western parts. The Welsh antiquarian Edward Llhuyd in his *Archaeologica Britannica: An Account of the Languages, Histories and Customs of Great Britain*, published in 1707, was the first to use the term in relation to the Atlantic seaboard of Britain and in respect of two families of languages: Goedelic – with its branches of Scottish and Irish Gaelic and Manx (sometimes known as Q Celtic) and Cymric or Brythonic – Welsh, Cornish and Breton (P Celtic).

We come here to one of the most significant, and on the face of it somewhat strange features of the use of the word Celtic, which is certainly true in terms of the phrase 'Celtic Christianity'. Despite the fact that the Celts are seen as having inhabited much of the continent of Europe, and Celtic art is particularly associated with finds in Austria and Switzerland, when used linguistically it applies much more narrowly just to the British Isles and not to Continental Europe. Its use is often extended to cover Brittany, sometimes to embrace Galicia in north east Spain and occasionally to include the Massif Central region of France. This almost exclusive focus on the British Isles is a marked feature of the concept of Celtic Christianity.

Indeed, 'Celtic' as it is generally used, and certainly when paired with Christianity has an even more specific focus. It usually refers to the 'Celtic fringe', the regions along the western seaboard of mainland Britain which, together with the island of Ireland, are seen as having been largely untouched by the Romans, wrongly as it happens, as recent research has suggested that the Romans penetrated further into Scotland and Wales than was long thought and also established settlements around Dublin. These areas have been seen as remote, marginal and liminal, their inhabitants constituting a faithful remnant who kept the flame of civilization and Christian culture alive through the so-called Dark Ages when the rest of Britain, like the rest of Europe, was in the grip of uncivilized pagan northern tribes like the Goths, Huns, Vandals, Angles, Saxons, Jutes and Vikings. This appealing romantic thesis has received much currency from proponents of the modern Celtic Christian revival, notably Thomas Cahill in his book *How the Irish Saved Civilisation* (1996). Fascination with the 'Celtic fringe' has been fuelled by the rise of national consciousness among the Irish, Scots, Welsh and Cornish which has helped to promote an image of the Celts, and not least the Christian Celts in these lands, as somehow marginalized and oppressed by their more powerful and authoritarian neighbours in England.

The identification of a specifically Celtic form of Christianity can really be traced back to the time of the Reformation. The first author that I can discover to use the word 'Celt' (or in his case *Celtae* because he was writing in Latin) in connection with religion was John Bale, a Carmelite friar who decisively rejected Roman Catholicism in the late 1530s and became an early and enthusiastic supporter of the Protestant reformers. His most important work, *The Actes of English Votaryes*, written during a period of exile in Antwerp in the early 1540s, presented an idyllic picture of a pure and primitive British church uncontaminated by Rome. In using the word *Celtae* to describe this church, he was suggesting a distinct Celtic (and British) Christian identity defined over and against Roman (and Continental) Christianity. This understanding of Celtic Christianity was shared by many other Protestant historians writing in the later sixteenth and seventeenth centuries, among them Archbishop Matthew Parker in his influential *De Antiquitate Britannicae Ecclesiae* (1572). It remains very influential even today, not least in encouraging the largely erroneous view that there was a distinct Celtic church in the British Isles standing consciously over and against the Roman church.

So how should Celtic Christianity be defined? Certainly not, as it sometimes seems to be, as a broad family or grouping of Christians like Catholics, Orthodox or Protestants. It was not a broad and distinct movement in the sense of these other groupings. Nor should it be seen as a separate denomination like Anglicanism, Presbyterianism or Methodism. There was no Celtic Church, as there is a Church of England, a Church of Scotland or an Episcopal Church of the USA. Rather we are dealing with something which is highly heterogeneous, with different expressions in different places and at different times. It is better defined geographically, linguistically and temporally, as the Christianity practiced by those living in the Celtic speaking regions of the British Isles over a particular timescale.

This is, in fact, the way that, for better or worse, the way the phrase is generally understood today. When people, whether scholars, popular authors, preachers or simply interested enthusiasts talk about 'Celtic Christianity' what they usually have in mind is the expression and practice of the Christian faith among the indigenous Celtic-speaking inhabitants of the British Isles between c.410 and 1066, the period which began with the departure of the Romans and ended with the arrival of Normans. Within this timescale, there is a particular emphasis on a perceived 'golden age' between the mid-fifth and mid-seventh centuries. This more limited period saw the flourishing of the best-known Irish and British saints, including Patrick, whose arrival in Ireland in or after 432 could be said to mark its start, Brigit, Brendan, Ninian, Columba, David, Columbanus and Aidan, whose death in 651 perhaps marks its end. It also saw the founding of the great monasteries at Clonmacnoise, Derry, Durrow, Glendalough, Iona, Llantwit Major and Lindisfarne. Often described as the 'age of saints', it seems to have combined missionary zeal, spiritual energy and simple faith in exceptional measure.

This widespread popular definition throws up its own considerable problems and questions. For a start the timescale envisaged in the first and wider definition is enormous: 650 years. A similar timescale would take us from 1370 to the present day – and no one would begin to see that as a distinct period or movement within our Christian history, encompassing as it does the later Middle Ages, the Reformation and the many different trends and movements in the eighteenth, nineteenth and twentieth centuries.

Even narrowing the definition of Celtic Christianity down to the 'golden age' from around 450 to 650 does not eradicate the difficulties. Several different influences were present then that were not remotely Celtic. The Roman influence was still very strong at the beginning of this period – it was through the Romans that Christianity came to Britain and even when the Roman legions left at the beginning of the fifth century to deal with the direct threat to Rome itself from invaders from northern Europe, many Roman influences remained. Indeed, Romano-British Christianity might be a much better term for the Christianity of these early centuries – it acknowledges the fact that both Patrick and Ninian appear to have come from mixed Roman-British stock. It is worth noting that the word 'Welsh' appears to have been an early English term meaning 'Romanized Celt'. During the latter part of this period, the impact of Anglo-Saxon Christianity was increasingly being felt, not least in Northumbria. The so-called 'Celtic Christianity' associated with the Northumbrian saints, Aidan, Oswald, Cuthbert, Hilda and Caedmon, and the Lindisfarne Gospels was in reality a fusion of Anglo-Saxon and Irish influences with the former contributing just as much as the latter.

It might also be noted here that it is very doubtful whether British and Irish Christians in the sixth and seventh centuries saw themselves as living in a golden age or regarded some of their contemporaries as saints. Certainly one of the very few contemporary accounts of the state of the church that has survived from this period, Gildas' *De Excidio Britanniae*, written in the mid to late sixth century, paints a picture of almost universal gloom and looks back longingly to the days of Roman occupation of Britain. For this Welsh monk at least, the Celticity of the early British church was a matter for lamentation rather than celebration.

A further question arises if the definition of Celtic Christianity is made, as scholars would like, on linguistic lines. In that understanding, is it properly understood as the Christian faith practised and articulated by those speaking Celtic languages, irrespective of any particular timescale? If so, then as well as the early poems and prayers from the Irish monasteries (many of which were actually written in Latin) we should include much later Gaelic and Irish prayers, of the kind collected in the late nineteenth century by Alexander Carmichael and Douglas Hyde, and Welsh language devotional poems right up to the present day.

Many of the enthusiasts for the modern Celtic Christian revival have in fact lumped together early material from the eighth and ninth centuries with much later poems and prayers coming from a thousand or more years later. I did this myself in *The Celtic Way*. I do so much more sparingly in this follow-up volume where I will be concentrating almost entirely on the early sources from the fifth to the eleventh centuries, only occasionally referencing and quoting the much later sources and not conflating what I have now come to realise are wholly different bodies of material, the earlier one from a largely monastic context and the later one predominantly from a popular folk tradition, with very different theological outlooks and spiritual perspectives.

Whether it is accurate or indeed helpful to use the phrase Celtic Christianity at all is a moot and much debated point. Many scholars prefer the term insular or indigenous Christianity or to talk about Christians of the Celtic speaking lands. There is a case for referring to early Irish Christianity, given that most of the early sources are Irish and that it was predominantly Irish monks who established monasteries in Scotland (the land of the Irish, according to the Romans who called the Irish 'Scoti'), Wales and northern England. Some historians prefer the broader term British Christianity. There may be something to be said for being even more specific and using terms like Columban Christianity which acknowledge the distinct monastic groupings and families. Perhaps it would be most accurate to talk in terms of the monastic Christianity of the British Isles in the early Middle Ages, since virtually all of our sources come comes from monasteries and virtually every Celtic saint, with the notable exception of Patrick, was a monk. But for better or worse, the term 'Celtic Christianity' is still in wide currency and in the popular imagination and it is probably best to stick with it, as I will, with some variations and qualifications, in this book.

So when I use the term 'Celtic Christianity' in the pages that follow, I am applying it to the native, indigenous Christian faith practised by those living in the British Isles in the early mediaeval period, and more specifically in those 'Celtic' speaking areas – the lands that would become Ireland, Scotland and Wales and also certain parts of England, notably Cumbria, Cornwall and other western areas before they were overrun by Angles, Saxons, Jutes and Vikings. It is, in other words, the Christianity of the Gaelic and Brythonic speaking population of the British Isles in the early mediaeval period.

The rest of this book will essentially focus on what we know and can say about Celtic Christianity using the definition above. Before we plunge into identifying and exploring its significant and dominant characteristics, it is worth pausing to consider what material we have to work on in the way of written sources and archaeological evidence. They are not hugely numerous and several of them are not contemporaneous with the events and characters that they describe. The evidence actually coming from the golden age is particularly scanty. But there is enough for us to identify some clear and characteristic themes.

3
The Sources

How can we best find out about Celtic Christianity as it has been defined in the last chapter? There are archaeological, artistic and literary sources to be explored. From the so-called 'golden age of the saints' we have relatively few contemporary sources, either written or archaeological. Most of the earliest lives of the fifth, sixth and seventh century saints were not written until as late as the eleventh or twelfth centuries – it is as though we were only now getting the first biographies of Luther or Calvin – and when they appeared they were hagiographies, not biographies, designed to show their subjects' miraculous and superhuman qualities and often produced as a public relations exercise to 'spin' the claims of a particular monastery. The high standing crosses that are so symbolic of Celtic Christianity did not start appearing until the late eighth century.

Christian leaders living in the Celtic speaking regions of the British Isles between the mid- sixth and mid-eighth centuries were probably too much involved in missionary work and setting up churches and monasteries and too preoccupied with thoughts of imminent judgement and the last days to reflect on their times or make beautiful and lasting artefacts. In a society in which literacy was still very limited, such literary production as did take place was largely confined to the basic biblical and liturgical texts needed to carry on monastic worship and an itinerant preaching and sacramental ministry. To some extent, this is a reflection of the provisionality which I discuss in the next chapter as one of the striking characteristics of the Celtic approach to faith and church. Early churches and monastic buildings were constructed out of wood or wattle and daub and have left far less lasting traces than the stone buildings of later centuries.

The main sources which have survived from the early Mediaeval period are listed and described briefly in this chapter. Virtually all of them come from monasteries – this is true not just of the liturgical books, penitentials and monastic rules but also of the saints' lives and early poems and prayers. The monastic scriptorium was where all these documents were made – the only place in this period where serious writing and copying was being done and books and illuminated manuscripts produced. The high standing crosses and liturgical artefacts like chalices, pattens and crucifixes were similarly carved and fashioned in monastic workshops and the earliest incised stones seem to have come from monastic sites.

The fact that almost everything that has come down to us from this period has this shared provenance reflects the huge importance that monasteries clearly played in the Christian life and witness of the Celtic speaking peoples of the British Isles in the early Middle Ages. They were in many ways the key institutions of both church and society and fulfilled numerous roles, which I have enumerated and discussed in both *The Celtic Way* and *Colonies of Heaven*. We need, however, to be careful that the monastic origin and context of almost all our sources for Celtic Christianity do not skew our view of it. There was clearly much Christian life, faith, witness and worship going on outside and beyond the monasteries. The fact is that we know almost nothing about it. We really have next to no idea what Christians believed or did in terms of worship or ritual outside and beyond the monastic ditches or *valli* in the scattered rural townships where most people lived. The first real substantial evidence for lay Christian faith and practice in the Celtic speaking parts of the British Isles does not come for another 1000 years or so when folklorists like Alexander Carmichael and Douglas Hyde in the late nineteenth century started collecting and transcribing the oral prayers, poems, chants and incantations of crofters and fisherfolk. The material which they assembled seems very distant indeed in theological outlook and overall tone from what came out of the early Mediaeval monasteries – it is altogether gentler, less sin-centred, less judgemental and more affirmative of both human nature and the natural world. We really have no means of knowing whether this kind of lay spirituality was a relatively modern phenomenon or whether it echoed themes and tendencies which were there a thousand years or more earlier in the so-called 'golden age' of Celtic Christianity and its aftermath.

So when we talk about 'Celtic Christianity', as the term is usually understood and has been defined in this book as the faith and practice of Christians in the Celtic speaking regions of the

British Isles in the early Middle Ages, we are really talking about monastic Christianity, at least in terms of the sources that we have available to us. This means that we are also talking about a very male-dominated Christianity – we have very few surviving sources from nunneries and female communities – and also about an essentially élitist approach to the faith. Monasteries were highly hierarchical communities, run often in an autocratic manner by their abbots and where the professed monks were seen as the *miles Christi*, the élite shock troops regarded as several notches above ordinary lay Christians in terms of their spirituality and witness to Christ. It also means that we are dealing with a particularly austere, ascetic and demanding understanding of the Christian faith. These points are extremely important to bear in mind when it comes to exploring the Celtic Way as it is presented in the second part of this book from the almost exclusively monastic sources that have come down to us

The rest of this chapter will outline the main sources in terms of their different categories, firstly archaeological and artistic and then literary. The main focus is on material from the early mediaeval period – i.e. the fifth to the twelfth centuries – but there is a final brief section on the much more modern material, largely from the late nineteenth century, represented in the *Carmina Gadelica* and other collections which have been so widely drawn on in the current revival.

1 EARLY MEDIAEVAL SOURCES

A) ARCHAEOLOGICAL AND ARTISTIC SOURCES

Buildings and crosses

The archaeological sources for the 'golden age' of Celtic Christianity are very scant. Throughout the period from the mid-fifth to the mid-seventh centuries and well beyond it, churches in the Celtic-speaking regions of the British Isles were not generally built out of stone. Bede comments on how rare Ninian's church at Whithorn, known as Candida Casa or the White House, was in being built of stone, 'using a method unusual among the Britons'. Because churches, like other monastic buildings, were built out of wood or were simple wattle and daub structures, virtually nothing of them has survived. In some cases it has been possible to apply radio carbon dating to wooden remains at monastic sites, like the burned hazel stakes thought to have been part of Columba's writing hut on Iona which were dated in 2017 to between 540 and 640. For the most part, however, all that remain are the outlines of the monastic ditches, or *valli*, and these can give us an idea of the size of monasteries and also sometimes hint, as at Iona, of earlier settlements on the same site. The earliest stone churches did not appear until the very end of the eighth century – there is a reference to one at Armagh in 789 – and even then they were few and far between.

The earliest more durable monuments of Celtic Christianity are the incised stones and grave slabs which are found especially in the west of Scotland but also across Ireland and Wales. Some possibly go back to the sixth century and they provide the most widespread evidence for early Christianity in the British Isles. Argyll has the biggest concentration in Scotland with more than 350 early mediaeval carved stones – over 100 on Iona alone – ranging in date from the seventh to the eleventh century. The earliest have the simple device of a cross incised on an existing standing stone or prominent piece of rock. These cross-incised stones were planted in particular places possibly to mark the boundaries of sacred enclosures like monasteries and churches, and also more commonly as grave markers. Among the earliest examples that can be accurately dated, and now on display in the museum behind Iona Abbey, is a stone which is thought to have marked the grave of Echoid Buide, king of Dal Riata, who died in 629. The designs on these stones gradually became more elaborate and ornate.

The beehive cells found at certain remote sites associated with hermits and ascetic monks seeking their desert places on islands like Skellig Michael off the southern coast of Ireland and the Garvellach islands south of Mull in the Firth of Lorne probably go back at least as far as the eighth century. On the island of Eileach an Naoimh, the southernmost of the Garvellach islands, are the ruins of a double beehive cell made of local sandstone slabs and consisting of two round inter-connecting chambers with thick walls. They are said to be part of a monastery established there by Brendan around 540. If that is indeed, the case, which is far from proven, then they are among the oldest church buildings anywhere in the British Isles. There is no written record of their existence before the ninth century when the monastery apparently fell victim to Viking raiders.

Perhaps the most distinctive icons of Celtic Christianity, the high standing ringed crosses found across Ireland, with the finest examples at Monasterboice and Moone, and also on Iona and Islay, mostly date from the mid-eighth to the early tenth century. There are thirty or so 'Scripture crosses', so called because they are engraved with depictions of Biblical scenes with the themes of judgment and sacrifice prominent. Jesus is usually depicted either as an infant with his mother or reigning in triumph as *Christus Victor*. Otherwise, the faces of the crosses are covered with the distinctive pattern of intertwining serpents and bosses, or with interlacing knotwork and key patterns. There are various theories as to the reasons for the erection of these crosses, many of which are sited within or close to monastic compounds. Could they be theological statements about God's power, markers of sacred space or of important graves, stations on pilgrimage ways or visual aids to prayer and worship? Welsh crosses, like the Nevern Cross in Pembrokeshire, seem to have come rather later, generally being dated from the late tenth and early eleventh centuries. Crosses erected from the thirteenth and fourteenth centuries onwards are much more likely to show harrowing depictions of Jesus on the Cross.

The distinctive round towers associated with several Irish monasteries, and also found in Brechin and Abernethy in Scotland, seem mostly to date from the ninth to the twelfth centuries. Their purpose is also uncertain. Possibly they were refuges to which monks could retreat in the face of attack or they may have been used for storing grain.

Early Christian artefacts
There are several surviving artefacts associated with worship in Irish monasteries most of which appear to date from the eighth century. They include the Ardagh Chalice, used for communion, the Athlone Crucifix depicting Christ triumphant on the Cross flanked by angels, the Tara brooch, possibly worn by an abbot, a king or a bishop, and the Derrynaflan hoard of silver altar plate which was hidden from Viking raiders in the ninth century. These are all fashioned in the distinctive style of Celtic metalworking found at Hallstat and La Tène.

Illuminated manuscripts

Illuminated manuscripts, which were produced by monks working alone in the monastic scriptoria, display similar interlacing knotwork and spiral patterns to those found on the high standing crosses. They also often depict numerous animals and birds. Most are either Psalters or Gospel books. The art of copying and illustrating the Psalms and the Gospels was seen as an aspect of the *lectio divina*, or meditation and contemplation on the Scriptures, to which the monks were called.

In *the Cathach of St Columba*, a Psalter which dates from c.600 and contains Psalms 32 to 105 in the Latin translation by Jerome, providing the earliest example of Irish Latin script, the decoration is limited to the first letter of each psalm. The Gospel books which appear somewhat later are much more lavishly illustrated. The three most important of these are the *Book of Durrow*, possibly dating from the late seventh century and produced on Iona, the late eighth or early ninth century *Book of Kells*, which is also thought to be a product of the Iona monastic scriptorium, and the *Lindisfarne Gospels* which were probably produced between 715 and 720 on Holy Island although there have been suggestions that they may have had an Irish provenance.

B) LITERARY SOURCES

Lives of Saints (Vitae Sancti)

These are a vital source but need to be treated with care – they are hagiographical rather than biographical, having been written, in many instances several hundred years after the death of their subjects, to edify and promote claims of a particular monastery rather than as a historical record. They have a formulaic quality, being closely modelled on the Gospels, especially the stories of Jesus' miracles, and also on the *Vitae* of pioneering Eastern and European saints, notably the *Life of Antony* by Athanasius and the *Life of Martin of Tours* by Sulpicius Severus.

The earliest sources on Patrick are found in the *Book of Armagh*, which was almost certainly compiled in the monastery in Armagh in the very early ninth century. It contains the earliest known text of the *Confessio* attributed to him, which if it is indeed genuine, about which there is some doubt, would represent one of the earliest surviving texts from the 'golden age' of Celtic Christianity and one of the very few pieces of autobiographical writing by a Celtic saint. It also includes lives of Patrick by Muirchu and Tírechán, both probably written in the late seventh century, and various other writings about Patrick as well as substantial portions of the New Testament. These texts are available in various modern versions.

Columba is highly unusual among Irish saints in having been written about very soon after his death, which occurred in 597. The *Amra Choluimb Chille* (Elegy on Colmcille) appears to have been written around 600 by Dallan Forgaill, having possibly been commissioned by Columba's cousin, Aéd, King of Tara. Some fifty years later Beccán mac Luigdech, a hermit linked with Iona, wrote two poems about Columba. These early eulogies in both their original Latin versions and modern English translations can be found with very useful commentaries in Tom Clancy and Gilbert Márkus' *Iona: The Earliest Poetry of a Celtic Monastery.* Adomnán's *Vita Columbae* (Life of Columba), probably written in the late 690s, is easily available in several modern editions, of which the best is probably that edited by Richard Sharpe and published by Penguin. A much later *Irish Life*, probably compiled in Derry in the later twelfth century, is first found in a fifteenth-century manuscript known as the *Leabhar Breac* (Speckled Book).

Much of what we know about many of the other Celtic saints from the 'golden age' comes from *Vitae* which were written up to 500 years or more after their deaths by monastic hagiographers between the eleventh and thirteenth centuries largely for propaganda purposes to bolster the claims of a particular monastery. There is, unusually, a life of Samson written in Brittany in the seventh century, but the earliest extant life of David was only written in the late eleventh century by Rhigyfarch. A poem detailing Ninian's miracles apparently written by a monk at Whithorn in the later eighth century survives in a single eleventh-century manuscript but the first prose life of Ninian was not written until the late twelfth century, probably by Aelred of Rievaulx.

Early histories of the church
De Excidio Britonum (On The Ruin of Britain), written by the Welsh monk Gildas around 540 AD, is one of the very few contemporary accounts of the state of the church in Britain which comes from the so-called 'golden age' of Celtic Christianity. As has already been

pointed out, it paints a gloomy picture and suggests that things were very much better in the days of Roman occupation.

The Venerable Bede's *Ecclesiastical History of the English Nation*, written around 730 in the Northumbrian monastery of Jarrow, is an important and relatively early source of information, albeit limited, on Ninian, Columba, Aidan and the early Irish church. Bede portrays the Synod of Whitby of 664 as a confrontation between Roman and Irish forms of Christianity, an interpretation which has hugely influenced subsequent writers. Several manuscript versions of his *History* have been dated to the late 730s and early 740s. There are numerous modern editions in English, including the Oxford World's Classics Edition edited by Judith McClure and Roger Collins.

Chronologies and annals, listing key events and dates, were compiled in monasteries. The most important and comprehensive are the *Annals of Ulster*, generally thought to preserve material originally written on Iona, which cover the period from 431 to 1540 and are found in manuscripts dating from the fifteenth and sixteenth centuries. It is difficult to establish exactly when they began to be compiled but it is generally agreed that from the mid- to late seventh century the *Annals* ceased being historical and retrospective and began recording contemporary events. They are particularly useful for establishing the succession of kings and abbots, but also record other noteworthy events.

Penitentials and monastic rules

The largest single category of manuscript sources that have come down to us from the golden age of Celtic Christianity are the *Irish Penitentials*, long lists of precise punishments prescribed for every conceivable lapse from the high standard of behaviour expected of those living under monastic discipline. Although the manuscripts containing these lists often date only from the twelfth or thirteenth centuries, the Penitentials themselves are generally agreed to have been drawn up many centuries earlier, the oldest probably being that attributed to Finnian, which is thought to have been compiled at Clonard in the late sixth century. A Welsh Penitential attributed to Gildas possibly dates from around the same period. The *Penitential of Columbanus* followed soon after in the very early seventh century. *Cummean's Penitential*, which probably dates from around 650, is unusual in surviving in two continental manuscripts from the ninth century as well as in a tenth-century collection of Penitentials.

Monastic rules, attributed to well-known Celtic saints like Columba and Columbanus and also to lesser known figures such as Ailbe, Ciarán and Comgall, and very strict and demanding in tone, are largely found in eleventh and twelfth-century manuscripts and although some may have sixth or seventh-century origins, it is generally agreed that these rules were not compiled by the saints whose names they carry, but rather by later abbots in the monastic families which they established.

Standing somewhere between the early Penitentials and the monastic rules is the *Aptigír Chrábaid*, or *Alphabet of Devotion*, attributed to Colmán mac Béognae, an Irish monk largely active in the late sixth century who founded the monastery of Lann Elo in County Offaly. A primer of religious life, drawing much on the writings of Cassian, it provides a series of detailed instructions about living a pure, balanced and holy life and strengthening the soul.

Collectio canonum hibernensis is an important book of canon law probably dating from the late seventh or early eighth century. Compiled in an Irish monastery from Biblical and patristic teaching and decrees from Irish synods, it is one of the first handbooks of canon law. Its 67 books range wide, covering legal regulations and precedents relating to monarchy and civic matters as well as to the church. Exacting and austere in tone, like the Penitentials and monastic rules, it extols virginity as the highest state of life for Christians to follow, with marriage being seen very much as a second best.

Biblical exegesis

Several early passages of Scriptural exegesis survive, notably of the Psalms. Among the earliest is a Hiberno-Latin commentary on Psalm 103 written around 700. Later commentaries include one on Psalm 118 dating from the tenth century.

Liturgical texts

Early liturgical material includes the *Antiphonary of Bangor*, of which the earliest manuscript version, dating from the late seventh century and now in the Ambrosian Library in Milan, comes from the monastery founded by Columbanus at Bobbio. It was probably copied there from a manuscript brought over from Bangor. It contains an order for the Mass, with little deviation from the Roman rite used across Western Europe, as does another seventh century manuscript of similar provenance, the *Bobbio Missal*. The *Stowe Missal*, which was probably compiled in the Irish monastery of Tallaght in the late eighth or early ninth century, is now in the Royal Irish Academy in Dublin, having for a time been in the private collection of the Marquis of Buckingham at Stowe House in Buckinghamshire. The most significant element added to the order for the Mass in the *Stowe Missal* is an opening litany which acknowledges the sinful state of the worshippers and seeks forgiveness, asking specifically for the prayers of a large number of named saints.

Other Irish litanies, probably dating back to the ninth century, are gathered in Charles Plummer's compilation *Irish Litanies: Texts and Translations* (1925). They include the *Litany of the Irish Saints* and the *Litany of Pilgrim Saints*, both long sets of prayers with repetitive responses, in which the themes of penitence and protection loom large.

Prayers and poems

The earliest source for many Irish prayers and poems, including *St Patrick's Breastplate*, is the *Liber Hymnorum*, a collection of 40 hymns in Latin and Irish. The oldest manuscript copy, now in Trinity College, Dublin, dates from the eleventh century. It is very difficult to establish the date of early Irish hymns, prayers and poems – *St Patrick's Breastplate* is often given an eighth-century dating but it could conceivably be earlier, although almost certainly not as far back as Patrick's own lifetime. The poem which is known to us as 'Be thou my vision' is first found in manuscripts now in the Royal Irish Academy which have been dated to the eighth century but there is some doubt about this. Early Latin prayers from Iona, often attributed to Columba, including the one probably most likely to have been written by him, the *Altus Prosator*, and also *Adiutor laborantium*, which is first found in an eleventh-century manuscript in Winchester, can be found both in their original Latin form and in translation in Clancy and Márkus' *Iona: The Earliest Poetry of a Celtic Monastery*. The classic anthology of early Irish poems remains Gerard Murphy's *Early Irish Lyrics*, first published in 1946 and reprinted numerous times since.

There are two main sources for early Welsh poems and prayers. The *Black Book of Carmarthen*, which exists in a thirteenth-century manuscript almost certainly compiled in a Cistercian monastery, contains monastic poems dating back to the ninth or tenth centuries. *The Book of Talieisin*, a fourteenth-century manuscript, possibly contains earlier poems. It has been suggested that some of those attributed to Taliesin praising Urien, a king of the Celtic kingdom of Rheged in Cumbria, may come from the sixth century. Both of these books contain pre-Christian as well as Christian material.

Sermons and stories

Almost the only sermons surviving from the so-called Golden Age of the Saints are those attributed to Columbanus, the sixth-century Irish missionary monk who set up monasteries across Europe, notably at Bobbio in Italy where he died in 615. The earliest manuscript editions are found in a library in Turin, having come there from Bobbio in the second half of the ninth century but texts of the sermons were available to the eighth-century Northumbrian anchorite, Alchfirth, who borrowed from them in his own writings. After meticulous examination of the texts, Clare Stancliffe has concluded that the sermons were definitely written by Columbanus and 'take their place as the only coherent exposition of Irish ascetic spirituality to have come down to us from the formative period of early Irish monasticism. They also provide us with an insight into the religious inspiration of one of Ireland's greatest and most forceful *peregrini*. (Lapidge 1997:199). An interesting collection of Hiberno-Latin homilies which seem to have served as model sermons and been widely used by preachers was probably originally compiled in Ireland in the late seventh or early eighth century. Its contents are helpfully summarized and analysed by Thomas O'Loughlin in Chapter 8 of his book, *Journeys on the Edges the Celtic Tradition*. Later sermons from ninth-century Wales, Cornwall and Ireland are gathered together in a Breton manuscript entitled *Catechesis Celtica*.

Among the best-known and most romantic epic stories about the exploits of a Celtic saint is the *Navigatio Sancti Brendani* (Voyage of St Brendan) which appears in more than 120 manuscripts dating from between the twelfth and fourteenth centuries and found in monastic libraries across Continental Europe. For a long time the story of the epic journey of this seventh-century monk from Clonfert and his companions across the ocean in search of the Isle of the Blessed was thought to be a product of the twelfth-century Renaissance which also gave rise to the legend of the Holy Grail. However, its date of composition was pushed back by the discovery of a tenth-century manuscript. Scholars are generally agreed that the story of Brendan's voyage was probably first written down by an Irish monk on the Continent. They differ as to whether the *Navigatio* represents a Christianising of the *immrama*, tales of fantastic journeys which seem to feature in pre-Christian Celtic oral tradition, and specifically of the *Voyage of Braan*, thought to date from 700, or whether the *immrama* may rather derive from Christian legends like the *Navigatio*. Jonathan Wooding and others have argued that the story of Brendan's voyage should in fact be read as an allegory of the monastic life, with its themes of perpetual exile and withdrawal from the world.

Theological work
There is little in the way of substantial systematic theological writing surviving from the insular Christian communities of the British Isles in the early mediaeval period. The only two theologians of note to come from this tradition are Pelagius (c.350-418), who pre-dated the golden age of Celtic Christianity, having lived in Britain or Ireland during the period of Roman occupation in the late fourth and early fifth century and John Scotus Eurigena, who comes very much at the end of the period, having lived in the ninth century.

Pelagius belongs very much to the ascetic and monastic tradition so dominant in Celtic Christianity, and especially in the sources available for exploring it. He came as a monk schooled in the harsh and austere disciplines of Celtic monasticism to Rome where he was almost certainly shocked by the decadence and wealth of the church and famously fell foul of Augustine of Hippo on the issues of predestination, original sin and the extent to which humans can achieve salvation partly through their own efforts rather than being utterly dependent on God's grace. He ended up in Egypt where he was probably much happier among the desert monks. Not many of his writings survive – we are largely dependent on Augustine's possibly distorted accounts of them – although there are extant letters which Pelagius apparently wrote, chiefly to women, extolling the virtues of virginity and chastity. He was condemned as a heretic by Pope Zosimus in 418. Pelagianism has at various times been seen as a particularly British heresy – including by the great twentieth-century theologian Karl Barth. It does seem to have been rife in the late 420s when Pope Celestine sent Germanus, Bishop of Auxerre, on a mission to Britain to counter its hold. In *The Celtic Way*, I made a lot of Pelagius and his representative status as an exponent of a benign view of human nature and creation. Many other writers have made similar claims. I am now rather less certain of whether Pelagianism, as it is usually understood, was a characteristic of Celtic Christianity in its golden age – the evidence, such as it is, in terms of prayers, sermons and other texts, would suggest rather the opposite. What is clear, though, is that Pelagius did articulate many of the dominant themes of Celtic monasticism, notably austerity, martyrdom, and a quest for puritanical perfectionism.

John Scotus Eurigena (c.810-877) was Irish – his last name means 'coming from Ireland' - but spent much of his time in Gaul where he seems to have done most of his theological writing. He was an important theologian, generally agreed to have produced the most distinctive systematic theology between Augustine and Aquinas. His reputation chiefly rests on two works, *Periphyseon*, or *De Divisione Naturae*, and his *Homily on the Prologue of St John's Gospel*, although he wrote much else. Both are strongly mystical in tone and very much in the Greek apophatic tradition, emphasizing the unknowability of God. Eurigena is associated with the doctrine of emanationism, understood as suggesting that all creation proceeds or emanates from God. His statements on creation are dense and ambiguous – he holds that God is simultaneously both present in all things and beyond all things – and it is difficult to establish how representative he was, but he does possibly exemplify a creation-centred strand in Celtic Christianity.

MORE MODERN SOURCES

In addition to the mediaeval sources listed above, there are other more modern sources which have provided much of the material used in the modern Celtic Christian revival and often feature in modern Celtic liturgies. They tend often to be conflated with and used alongside the early mediaeval material - I did this in *The*

Celtic Way - but their whole tone is very different, not least because they come from non-monastic sources and represent the thoughts, prayer and practice of largely uneducated lay Christians living in remote rural communities.

Easily the most important and the most often quoted of these more modern sources are the *Carmina Gadelica* or *Songs of the Gael* compiled in the late nineteenth century by Alexander Carmichael and published in six volumes between 1900 and 1971. Some Celtic scholars have been uneasy at the extent to which Carmichael may have doctored and altered the raw material that he collected in the form of Gaelic prayers, blessings and incantations from Hebridean crofters and fisherfolk when he translated them to make more poetic and flowing verses. I am myself inclined to believe that they are authentic, but questions remain as to how far back they go in terms of an oral folk tradition. Carmichael commented in the preface to the first volume of *Carmina* that 'some of the hymns may have been composed within the cloistered cells of Derry and Iona' in the time of Columba. In fact, they are so radically different in tone and theology from the early Iona material that it seems likely their provenance is much later. They display a great sense of intimacy with the Celtic saints, who are often invoked, a closeness to nature and a panentheistic theology where God is seen as being in everything. The overall tone is much gentler and more pagan-tinged than that of the surviving early mediaeval monastic material. Extracts from the *Carmina*, sometimes versified or otherwise adapted, have appeared in numerous paperback anthologies of Celtic prayers and the whole collection is conveniently presented with Carmichael's notes in a single volume published by Floris Press.

Less often quoted are *The Religious Songs of Connaught*, a collection of Irish prayers, charms, blessing and curses collected by Douglas Hyde, a leading enthusiast in the late-nineteenth and early-twentieth-century Celtic revival, and first published in 1906. The early twentieth century also saw the appearance of important anthologies of earlier Irish material, notably Kuno Meyer's Selections from *Early Irish Poetry* (1911) and Eleanor Hull's *The Poem Book of the Gael* (1912) which was notable for presenting the first appearance in verse of 'Be thou my vision'. Subsequent anthologies mixed early and much later material. A pioneer of this approach was A.P.Graves' *A Celtic Psaltery* (1917) in which 'lays of the Irish saints' and 'lays of monk and hermit' rubbed shoulders with Welsh poems from the Book of Carmarthen, eighteenth-century evangelical hymns from the Highlands and verses from the *Carmina Gadelica*.

This pick and mix approach, involving the juxtaposition of old and relatively recent material from Gaelic and Welsh, has characterized many of the more recent anthologies of Celtic Christianity. A good example from the early days of the modern revival is *Threshold of Light: Prayers and Praises from the Celtic Tradition*, edited by A.M. Allchin and Esther de Waal, first published in 1986, in which mediaeval Irish and Welsh poems stand side by side with eighteenth-century Welsh hymn texts, material from the *Carmina Gadelica* and poems by twentieth-century Welsh authors like Euros Bowen, Saunders Lewis and D.Gwenallt Jones. The unifying theme here, as in other modern anthologies of Celtic Christianity, has been texts written in Celtic languages (of which Welsh has been the richest and the most quoted in the twentieth century), always presented in translation. There are grounds for seeing the Welsh language as having a distinctive tradition of praise and blessing which can be traced right through from seventh to twenty first century but there are clear pitfalls inherent in conflating material from such very different and widely separated eras and trying to impose a continuity and to suggest a seamless and unbroken stream of Celtic Christian consciousness across fifteen centuries or so.

Part 2

Exploring the Way

Now that we have cleared the Celtic Way of the dense undergrowth of misconceptions and romantic accretions which has cluttered it for so long, what is left? A careful re-examination of the sources that have come down to us from the so-called 'golden age of Celtic Christianity' throws up a number of recurring themes and tendencies which are clearly apparent, striking and distinctive, if not necessarily unique. This central section of the book uncovers and explores twenty-one such themes, all beginning with the letter P and grouped under the headings of Marks of the church and expressions of faith; Attributes of God; Appropriate human responses; and Ways to follow. They can, perhaps, be taken as the key beliefs and practices of Celtic Christianity.

4

Marks of the Church and Expressions of Faith

1 PRAYERFUL

Monastic life is soaked in prayer. So it is no surprise to find that the monks of early Mediaeval Ireland, Scotland and Wales spent a good part of their days, and several hours every night, engaged in this activity both corporately and individually. Prayer was indeed at the very centre of their vocation, their faith and their witness.

The lives of several Celtic Saints suggest that they took very seriously St Paul's injunction in 1 Thessalonians 5:17 to 'pray continually'. Samson's biographer noted that 'neither by day nor by night did he cease from conversation with God, spending the whole day working with his hands and praying, and the whole night in mystical interpretations of Scripture'. According to Adomnán, Columba 'could not spend even a single hour without attending to prayer or reading or writing'. Patrick wrote in his autobiographical *Confessio* that in one day he would say around a hundred prayers and nearly the same number during the night and that 'come hail, rain or snow, I was up before dawn to pray'. His biographer Muirchu suggests that in later life Patrick was even more fervent in prayer, praying no less than 100 times in each hour of the day and of the night. Muirchu also noted that at every cross that Patrick saw as he travelled, he would get down from his chariot and turn towards it in order to pray. Rhigyfarch's *Life of David* portrays the monks in David's monastery spending three hours every evening after their meal in 'vigils, prayers and genuflections'. Rising at cockcrow, 'they apply themselves to prayer and genuflections and spend the rest of the night till morning without sleep'. Irish monastic rules emphasized the central importance of prayer. The Rule of Colmcille enjoined the monks following it to 'pray constantly for those who annoy you' and urged them that 'the extent of your prayer should be until tears come'. The art of copying and illuminating Gospel books and Psalters, usually carried out alone over many months, was seen as an act of prayer and the finished manuscripts were regarded like icons as a portal for prayer.

While the monks were called to undertake three labours – prayer, manual work and reading - there was a clear sense in which prayer dominated and also permeated the others. Monks were expected to pray while engaged in work with their hands and their reading, *lectio divina*, had an essentially devotional and prayerful character although it was seen as important in its own right and the balance of the three daily occupations was regarded as important. When a teacher named Daircellach approached the wise early-eighth-century Irish abbess, Samhthann, and told her that he was proposing to give up study in order to give himself wholly to prayer, she reportedly replied, 'What then can steady our mind and prevent it from wandering if you neglect spiritual study?'

Monks gathered for prayer in the simple wooden church at the centre of every monastic compound five times during the day, beginning at dawn with matins (also known as prime), followed by terce at the third hour after sunrise, sext at mid-day, nones in mid-afternoon and vespers in the evening. During the night there were three further shorter services (at nightfall, at midnight and towards daybreak) and vigils. Alongside these corporate acts of worship, monks spent long hours in the church or in their cells in silent and solitary prayer, sometimes lying on the floor or standing with their arms outstretched in what was known as the cross vigil. When a monk questioned Abbess Samhthann as to whether one should pray lying down, sitting or standing, she is said to have replied, 'In every position should one pray'.

Prayer was an attitude of mind. It arose spontaneously, coming out of a conviction similar to that expressed powerfully in the twentieth century by the Austrian Jewish philosopher Martin Buber that God is not so much to be expressed as addressed. The writings which have survived from the insular Celtic-speaking Christian communities of the British Isles in the early mediaeval period suggest that they did not go in for abstract theological treatises and discussions about the Divine nature and being, but preferred rather to address God directly through prayer, praise and petition. Several of the prayers that have come down to us from the 'golden age of Celtic Christianity' are deeply personal, like *Adiutor laborantium* attributed to Columba and *St Patrick's Breastplate*. Others have a broader, more cosmic and detached feel, like the *Altus Prosator*, also attributed to Columba.

As with so much else, it is difficult to know what happened outside and beyond the confines of the monasteries. It has been suggested that the high standing crosses were prayer stations where the faithful would gather, meditate on the Biblical stories portrayed on their faces and pray together. Much later sources, notably the late-nineteenth-century *Carmina Gadelica*, suggest a prolific lay folk culture of prayers, charms, incantations and blessings, some almost pagan in form, full of physical and natural imagery and often invoking the Celtic saints. Whether this kind of rich vernacular lay prayer culture existed in the early Mediaeval period is much less certain – we have no clear evidence that it did so.

2 PSALM-CENTRED

Chanted, recited, copied, studied and prayed, the psalms were central to the spiritual and devotional life of Irish monasteries. Singing them, almost certainly antiphonally to Gregorian-like tones, was the main feature of the regular daily and nightly offices. Irish monks chanted more psalms in their services than later continental Benedictine monks and so got through the full cycle of 150 more rapidly. They must have come to know them by heart. Those whom they evangelized, when they went out with their Gospel books and Psalters attached to their belts, must also have become very familiar with them. Verses and images from the Psalms crop up again and again in early Irish and Welsh poems and prayers. They were second only to the Gospels in terms of their theological influence and arguably even more pervasive in terms of their imagery.

It is important to point out that Celtic Christianity was not unique in this respect. It was a requirement for priests throughout the early mediaeval Latin church that they were *psalterati*, able to recite psalms by heart. Work by recent scholars has shown that the psalms were equally central in Anglo-Saxon worship. Nonetheless the references to the importance of the psalms in early Irish and Welsh sources are particularly striking and numerous. There were very detailed rules for the number of psalms to be chanted each day in the monasteries. The rule of Columbanus laid down that through the week 12 psalms should be chanted at nightfall, 12 at midnight and 22 towards morning. The weekend tally was higher. During the summer, between 24 June and 1 November, 75 psalms were to be sung antiphonally on both Saturday and Sunday nights so that the whole Psalter was covered over the weekend. During the winter months, this number was reduced to 36, the same as on weekday nights. Rhigyfarch's life of David speaks of the monks in his monastery being summoned by evening bell to leave their work and make their way in silence to the church. 'When they had sung the psalms, in unity of heart and voice, they devoutly remained on bended knees until the appearance of the stars of heaven marked the close of the day'.

As well as pointing to the importance of the communal chanting of the psalms in worship, the lives of the saints also often describe them being read, recited and meditated on individually. Maedoc, a seventh-century Irish monk, is said to have subsisted on barley bread and water for seven years and to have recited 500 psalms each day during this period. According to Muirchu's life, Patrick used to recite all the Psalms when he was travelling along the road and also when he was staying anywhere overnight. There are numerous stories telling of Columba's attachment to the Psalms. One, found in the *Leabhar Breac*, suggests that his constant boyhood visits to the tiny church of Tulach Dubhglaise (Temple Douglas) close to his birthplace to recite the psalms led local children to give him the name Columcille, the dove of the church. There is another story that when on one occasion Cruithnechan, the elderly priest to whom he was fostered as a boy, was unable to remember the 100th Psalm when asked to officiate at a holy festival, his young pupil, who had only just mastered the alphabet, stepped in and recited it perfectly. Adomnán writes of Columba singing Psalm 44 very loudly outside the palace of the pagan Pictish king, Brude. He also movingly describes the aged saint copying out the Psalter in his cell in the last hour of his life, stopping when he had reached the verse in Psalm 34 which says that 'those who wait on the Lord will not want for anything that is good'. The *Old Irish Life* portrays Columba going down to the shore on Iona in the early hours of the morning, after sleeping briefly on the floor of his cell with a stone for his pillow, and chanting all 150 Psalms (the three fifties) before daybreak:

The three fifties, a heavy burden,
Throughout the night, great was the pain,
In the sea alongside Scotland,
Before the sun would rise.

Some of the earliest surviving artefacts from the golden age of Celtic Christianity are transcriptions of the psalms. Possibly the very earliest extant example of Irish handwriting is to be found in some verses scratched with a metal stylus on to the wax covering a set of wooden tablets preserved in the peat of Springmount Bog and dating from around 600. As Michelle Brown observes, 'perhaps the traveling priest who owned them became so absorbed in learning the psalms on his journey, as many monastic rules of life advocated, that he took a tumble into the bog and lost his precious tablets' (Brown 2006:114). The *Cathach of Columba*, dating from the same period, and containing a transcription of Jerome's translation of Psalms 32 to 105, is the oldest extant example of Irish Latin script and the earliest illuminated manuscript. It is just possible that it was the work of Columba himself, maybe even the infamous copy which he made of the Psalter belonging to Finnian of Moville which led him to be accused of plagiarism and to be banished from Ireland.

The psalms impacted deeply on the spirituality and theology of those who knew them so well. Their imagery of rocks, mountains, trees and other natural features helped to form and colour the intense physicality of Celtic Christianity. They played a significant role in emphasizing the protective power of God and the themes of praise and penitence. Psalms of lament were every bit as influential and important as psalms of praise. A letter attributed to Pelagius makes much of how they should be approached in a spirit of penitence: 'when you repeat a psalm, consider whose words you are repeating and take pleasure in the contrition in your soul rather than in the sweetness of that ruling voice. For God gives his approval to the psalm-singer's tears rather than the charm of his voice'. (Rees 1991:87)

Psalms continued to be extremely important in Gaelic culture and worship and remain so today. They were a major influence behind the spiritual songs of the great Gaelic evangelical bards in the Scottish highlands like Donald Buchanan in the eighteenth century and Peter Grant in the nineteenth. For many Presbyterians in the Scottish Highlands and islands, especially in the Free Churches, chanting the psalms unaccompanied and led by a precentor is still at the heart of Sunday worship. In that respect, one of the key marks of the church among the Gaelic speaking Christians of the early Middle Ages remains a distinguishing characteristic of their successors today.

3 POETIC

The poetic quality of the prayers from early mediaeval insular Christian sources is often singled out by modern enthusiasts for Celtic Christianity. It suggests a faith conceived and expressed as much through the imagination as the intellect, in images rather than in concepts. I made much of this in *The Celtic Way* with a chapter on 'The Power of Imagination' in which I quoted Martin Reith, a priest in the Scottish Episcopal Church, who encapsulated the difference between early Celtic and contemporary Western Christianity as being the contrast between 'twopence coloured poetry and penny plain prose' (Bradley 1993:95). Much of the modern appeal of Celtic prayers, whether from early sources or more recent ones like the *Carmina Gadelica*, lies in their deeply poetic quality. Generally short, rhythmic and packed with vivid images, they seem very different from the more leaden, prosy and lengthy prayers to which we have been subjected and grown accustomed in both Roman Catholic and Protestant worship.

There is no doubt that intense exposure to the psalms was an important factor in giving a rhythmic, poetic quality to the early prayers and liturgical material which were largely, if not exclusively, the work of monks. Their influence pervades almost all the writings that have come down to us from the early mediaeval monasteries of the British Isles. Other deeper cultural factors undoubtedly also played a part. Pre-Christian Celtic society accorded a high role to poets. In Ireland the *filid*, or bards, were a much venerated and respected caste regarded as guardians of the great oral tradition of folk-lore and heroic legend which sustained the community and provided its roots. Often attached to royal households, the *filid* effectively constituted a distinct profession living off public subsidy. The highest order of Irish poets, who took the title *ollam*, enjoyed a status comparable to that of a bishop or petty king. The same was true in Wales where the highest grade of poets were known as *pencerdd*. The coming of Christianity did not overthrow this reverence for poets and their craft although it did bring about an important change in replacing an oral with a written culture. The monks who toiled away in the monastic scriptoria did not just copy and illustrate psalters and Gospel books. They absorbed the bardic culture and to a large extent took over the bardic role, writing down, for the first time, poems and stories about heroes and battles from the pre-Christian past which had previously been passed down by word of mouth.

A story in a late edition of the old Irish life of Columba suggests that he went from Iona to the convention of Druim Ceat in Ireland in 575 specifically to defend the order of *filid* and oppose their expulsion by their royal paymasters. The high king of Ireland, Aed, was apparently keen to banish the poets not just because of the cost of their salaries and retinues but because of the 'multitude and sharpness of their tongues' and the satire which they had directed against him. Columba seems to have defended the poets and saved them from banishment. It has been suggested that the poetic eulogy *Amra Cholumb Chille*, written soon after the Saint's death, was composed in gratitude to Columba for his defence of the *filid*. A line in the *Amra* stating that Columba 'went with two songs to heaven' has generally been taken to indicate that he wrote poems or hymns himself. This idea is supported by the tradition that Gemmán, mentioned by Adomnán as Columba's teacher while he was a deacon at Leinster, was a bard who inspired his young charge with the rich treasury of pre-Christian Irish verse. Adomnán also refers to 'a book of the week's hymns written out by Columba in his own hand' although it is not clear if these were his original compositions or merely copies. Many poems and hymns have been attributed to Columba, of which the most likely to come from his own hand are *Altus Prosator* and *Adiutor Laborantium*, both of which are quoted in the next chapter of this book.

Whether or not Columba wrote these and the other poems attributed to him, and whether or not Patrick was the author of the Breastplate prayer that bears his name, the fact that these and other early poems were attributed to the Celtic saints shows how much they were valued. It also indicates a broader appreciation of poetic imagery, metaphor and imagination. The Celtic saints were associated with an approach to expressing and explaining the mysteries of the Christian faith through story, symbol and verse rather than through intellectual proposition, argument, concept and debate. This is vividly illustrated in the way that Patrick is depicted in popular legend and tradition as explaining the doctrine of the Trinity by picking up a three leaved clover rather than by recourse to lengthy abstract theological argument in the manner of the early Greek fathers hammering out the creeds of the church. Several historians of Irish monasticism have pointed to the fact that it did not develop a theology of its own in the philosophical or systematic sense, but rather assimilated and adopted the Celtic druidic, bardic approach of emphasizing the affective and poetic over the cognitive (see Thom 2006:20). Brendan Bradshaw has drawn attention to the lack of formal and systematic theology in the monasteries and observed that 'early Christian Ireland teemed with scholars, as it teemed with saints, but the scholars were manuscript copiers, rhetoricians, computists, skilled in Latin and biblical exegetes; they were not, in any serious way, philosophers or theologians' (Bradshaw 1989:20). In Noel O'Donoghue's words, they preferred 'lyrical speculation' and 'the light of imagination' (O'Donoghue 1993: 31). This approach put a premium on the role of the poet.

Oliver Davies has commented that Celtic Christianity 'affords a special value to the creativity of the poet as one who both instructs the people and speaks before God on their behalf ... It is above all here, in the implicit notion of a poetic priesthood in which the poet – touched by a particular grace – speaks in and for the spiritual community, that we find the most distinctive aspect of the Welsh tradition' (Davies 1996:144). The Welsh Christian tradition is indeed the most affirmative of the priestly role of poets. There is evidence that the bardic tradition was assimilated even earlier and more thoroughly into Welsh Christianity than into Irish Christianity. This may explain the particularly rich corpus of Christian poetry in both the *Book of Taliesin* and the *Black Book of Carmarthen*, the latter of which includes a poem commending 'listening to the songs of clear-speaking poets' as being among the devotional practices required of a pious soul. Davies notes that the positive view of poetry taken in both early Welsh and Irish Christianity was in stark contrast to the general attitude of the mediaeval Catholic church which was hostile especially to poetry in the vernacular. He writes that 'it is not easy to point to other non-Celtic European cultures in which poetry has so consistently served as a kerygmatic, confessional and devotional focus for the spiritual life of a community, although there are traces of a similar function in the earliest Anglo-Saxon poetry of Caedmon and Cynewulf' (Davies 1996:116).

This point about Anglo-Saxon poetry is well made – one only has to think of the Dream of the Rood – and underlines the wider truth that in this as in other respects Celtic and Anglo-Saxon Christianity were much closer than proponents of a distinctive 'Celtic spirituality' have tended to make out. But it is also right to single out this aspect of Welsh Christianity as being particularly distinctive and long-lasting. There is a clear and unbroken tradition of praise poetry written in the Welsh language, which runs from one of the earliest surviving examples of written Welsh, a note in the margin of a ninth-century manuscript that 'it is not too great a toil to praise the Trinity' to the work of twentieth-century poets like D. Gwennalt Jones and Euros Bowen. Underlying all these poems is a conviction that the poet has the priest-like role of blessing in its original meaning of speaking good things, declaring the goodness that is latent in the world and offering up a sacrifice of praise and thanksgiving to God. This important and distinctive Welsh expression of a wider Celtic Christian theme is explored in A.M. Allchin's *Praise Above All* (1991) and B. O'Malley's *A Welsh Pilgrim's Manual* (1989).

4 PURITANICAL PERFECTIONISM

There was a very strong puritanical strain in Celtic Christianity. It was allied to a striving for spiritual perfection and a belief that following Christ involved living a life of extreme asceticism and self-mortification. Strongly influenced by the austere ascetic disciplines and practices associated with the Desert Fathers, hagiographers depict the Celtic Saints as superhuman figures not just in terms of their performance of miracles and ability to prophesy but also in their capacity for mortifying the flesh and devoting themselves almost continually to harsh religious exercises and disciplines to the virtual exclusion of any pastimes or distractions. Adomnán's comment about Columba is typical – 'he was ceaselessly occupied with the untiring labours of fasts and vigils, day and night, any of which works would seem to be humanly impossible'. Irish monastic rules and Penitentials enjoined similarly punishing regimes of self-mortification bordering on the masochistic.

It is important to remember that these sources are all coming from a monastic context. Monks and nuns subject themselves intentionally to lives of poverty, chastity and obedience, consciously forswearing worldly pleasures, comforts and distractions. That said, there is a particular harshness about the disciplines imposed on Celtic monks. The rules and regulations to which they were subjected were noticeably more demanding than those applied, for example, in the Rule of Benedict which was more relaxed. Benedictine monks were able to enjoy eight hours of uninterrupted sleep, a luxury denied to those in Irish monasteries who were woken three times during the night for vigils. The daily rations which Benedict allowed each monk included a pound of bread, a dish of fruit or young vegetables and more than half a pint of wine, a menu which, in the words of John Ryan, author of a classic work on Irish monasticism, 'would have sounded incredible to Irish ears' (Ryan 1992:410-11). The Rule of Columbanus, by contrast, was unequivocal that 'the chief part of the monk's rule is mortification', while the Rule of Columcille ended with this chilling peroration:

> The extent of your prayer should be until tears come.
> The measure of your work should be to labour until tears of exhaustion come.
> The limit of your labour, or of your genuflections in the event that tears do not come, should be perspiration.

The *Vitae* of the saints give a similar picture of severe austerity. Rhigyfarch's *Life of David* noted that the clothing of monks in his monastery 'was humble, mostly skins and their food 'bread and vegetables seasoned with salt'. David's own daily routine was described in similarly puritanical terms: 'After Matins he proceeded alone to commune with the angels, and then immediately sought out cold water where he remained for a sufficient length of time to quell the ardour of the flesh' (Davies 1999:200). It may well have been this practice that earned David the nickname *Aquaticus* although it may equally well have been his teetotalism. Other Celtic monks similarly forswore the demon drink and abstained from alcohol – there are stories of Irish ascetics who drank nothing but water and ate nothing but grass. David was by no means alone in regularly immersing himself in cold water for a considerable period each day. Other Welsh saints were described as wading out into the sea and standing up to their waists, and in some cases up to their chests, chanting psalms. Muirchu described Patrick venturing out nightly to stand in the middle of a cold river for solitary prayer. His young companion Beningus accompanied him one night but found the river unbearably cold and abandoned the vigil after just a few minutes. Bede famously described Cuthbert (strictly speaking an Anglo-Saxon rather than a Celtic saint) going down to the sea below the monastery at Coldingham:

> Wading into the depths till the waves swelled up to his neck and arms, he kept his vigil through the dark with chanting voiced like the sea. As the twilight of dawn drew near, he waded back up the beach, and kneeling there, again began to pray; and as he prayed, straight from the depths of the sea came two four-footed beasts which are called by the common people otters.
>
> These, prostrate before him on the sand, began to busy themselves warming his feet with pantings, and trying to dry them with their fur; and when this good office was rendered, and they had his benediction, they slipped back again beneath their native waters. He himself returned home, and sang the hymns of the office with the brethren at the appointed hour.

It is conceivable that this commonly reported practice among both Celtic and Anglo-Saxon saints of standing for long periods in cold water was not just motivated by austere asceticism. A Swedish biochemist suggested to me when I described it during a course on Celtic Christianity on Iona that it would have probably been the most effective way of getting rid of lice and other infestations. Maybe those who went in for frequent immersion in cold water were, indeed, seeking to rid themselves of parasites rather than sins but the practice was certainly written up by hagiographers as an exercise in puritanical asceticism.

Of course, Saints' *Vitae* and monastic rules express ideals and cannot be taken necessarily as evidence for what actually happened in the early Celtic monasteries. However, they do express a distinct theology rooted in asceticism and owing much to the influence of the Desert Fathers of Egypt and Syria. At the heart of this theology was an overwhelming desire both to conform and witness to Christ. The Greek word for witness is *marturos* which has given us the word martyr with its connotations of suffering and self-sacrifice. These connotations were certainly very much in the minds of Irish monks who valued and sought to practise three specific types of martyrdom, both as witnesses to the earnestness of their Christian faith and as paths to lives of perfection which would fit them for heaven. These were first described in one of the oldest surviving examples of continuous Irish prose, dating from around 700 and copied into a book commissioned by the Bishop of Cambrai. The highest form, red martyrdom, or dying for the faith, was not usually an option in an age when Christians were not generally persecuted, although some monks did make this ultimate sacrifice in the face of Viking attacks. White martyrdom involved abandoning home, family and country to travel to foreign lands as a pilgrim. Green martyrdom, the most widely practised of the three forms, involved a life of purgation and penitence based on obedience, abstinence, fasting and prayer. It envisaged the core of the monk's calling in terms of ceaseless penitential activity, renunciation of sin and mortification of the flesh in order to achieve Christian perfection and be fit for heaven. Adomnán described this approach in a nutshell in his summing up of Columba in the preface to his *Vita*: 'With God's help he had kept his body chaste and his mind pure and shown himself, though placed on earth, fit for the life of heaven'.

There is much in this approach, and the practices which it engendered, that would strike us today as distinctly masochistic. That element is clearly there in the *Alphabet of Devotion*, generally taken to be a primer for the dedicated religious life, when it describes 'the four securities of the sons of life' as 'the wearing away of the passions, fear of the pains, love of the sufferings, belief in the rewards'. It is impossible to avoid the sense here of a positive courting of sufferings and pains, however unpleasant they be. There is more than a hint, too, of a doctrine of Christian perfectionism. What Catherine Thom notes about Columbanus is true of many other monks and saints as they are portrayed in their *Vitae*:

> His initial response to the call to leave mother and motherland shows a man of action who is obsessed with the search for Christian perfection regardless of the personal hardship. His lifestyle gave concrete evidence of the ascetical theology that

underpinned it: an ascetic regime that included prayer, fasting and behaviour that 'incarnated' these values and practices. Like many of his Celtic forebears, his view of life is that of a battlefield and so the spiritual quest is easily seen as a battle in which the foe is the selfish human spirit, and the weapons are the penances and ascetical practices.

(Thom 2006: 55)

There is an undoubted spiritual élitism at work here which goes with both the doctrine of perfectionism and the battlefield and military metaphors so often employed in early Celtic texts. It makes uncomfortable reading for those who would see Celtic Christianity as essentially egalitarian, non-hierarchical and anti-militaristic. Monks were regarded as a spiritual élite, the *miles Christi*, soldiers of Christ and crack troops in the war to subdue the flesh, renounce the world and do battle with the forces of evil. They were also seen as being closer to Christ and nearer to heaven than those leading more worldly lives outside the monasteries. Commenting on what he calls a 'two-tiered approach to the Christian life and to salvation', Hugh Connolly has written 'one has, at times, the distinct impression, on reading the early Celtic penitential and spiritual literature, that Irish churchmen saw themselves as something of an élite sub-group of Christians' (Connolly 1995:182). This sense of spiritual hierarchy is clearly expressed in the strict rules which governed exactly who could venture where inside the monastic enclosures.

There ought to be two or three boundaries around a holy place: the first, into which we allow no one at all to enter except the saints, since laymen do not draw near to it, nor women, but only clergy; the second, into whose streets we allow crowds of rustic folk to enter who are not much given to wickedness; the third, into which we do not forbid lay homicides and adulterers to enter, by commission and custom.

(Clancy & Márkus 1995: 20)

How far did this puritanical perfectionism extend to those who were not living under monastic discipline? A Welsh poem, *The Advice of Addaon*, possibly dating from the eleventh century, and apparently directed as much at lay Christians as those under monastic vows, listed the activities that profit the soul as saying prayers, building up peace, feeding the hungry, clothing the naked, and 'avoiding too much sleep, drunkenness and sipping of mead, and too much pandering to the body'. This seems to shift the emphasis away from extreme self-mortification and more towards practical good works. Nonetheless it is difficult to avoid the conclusion that in the early period at least, an austere world-denying puritanism was advocated as the correct Christian way not just for monks and priests but for all who sought to follow Christ. Such an attitude is certainly clearly evident in the sermons of Columbanus, which seem to have been directed primarily at a lay audience. They preached again and again about the dangers of being distracted by the pleasures and delights of this world which is essentially just a road leading to the heavenly home where our thoughts should be focused (see page 61). The closing couplet of the *Altus Prosator*, attributed to Columba, asks 'Who can please God in the final time?' and responds 'only those who have contempt for the present world'.

A doctrine of puritanical perfectionism is very clearly worked out in the writings of Pelagius. Himself a monk schooled in the austere teaching and practices of Irish monasticism and deeply influenced by the extreme asceticism of the Desert Fathers, he was clearly troubled by the decadence and laxity that he found in the church in Rome. Pelagius emphasized behaviour and conduct, which seemed for him to be every bit as important as belief and faith, if not more so. This led him to expound a theology of perfectionism, which went beyond the notion of sanctification found in Charles Wesley's observation in 'Love Divine, all loves excelling' that humans can in this life be 'changed from glory into glory, till in heaven we take our place'. Pelagius' extant letters, which were mostly directed to women, extolled a life of perfection and especially commend the qualities of virginity and chastity, although he also makes a lot of practical good works. He suggested that it was possible to live a life without sin and wrote of 'ordering the perfect life', telling one of his correspondents, the 14-year-old Demetrias, to embrace 'the counsel of perfection' and 'direct your mind's attention to complete moral perfection and prepare yourself to lead a heavenly life for a heavenly reward' (Rees 1991:62).

Here, perhaps, we have the root of Pelagianism and the reason why it was seen as a heresy. It was not so much about free will versus determinism, or the innate goodness of humanity, created in the image of God, over and against original sin. Rather it was

Pelagius' conviction that it was possible to live without sin and that the way to get to heaven was by joining the spiritual élite of monks, virgins and others living lives of absolute puritanical austerity. In the words of B.R. Rees, perhaps the leading modern authority on Pelagius, 'Pelagianism was not intended to be a prop for the weary and faint-hearted but a school for would-be saints…The Pelagians, like the early Syriac Church, saw asceticism and austere morality as essential ingredients of everyday life and the unremitting quest for perfection.' (Rees 1991: 9, 23)

Celtic Christianity, certainly in its monastic incarnation which is what we know most about, was all about austere asceticism and self-mortification, celibacy, virginity and spiritual warfare. Of course, there were other elements too, like the penitence and poverty which will be explored in Chapter 6. The overwhelming impression given by the surviving monastic sources in the early period, the so-called golden age, however, is of an overriding puritanical perfectionism which encouraged a kind of spiritual élitism. It presents a forbidding and not altogether attractive picture.

5 PHYSICAL

There is something very physical about Celtic Christianity in its golden age. It is there in the austere practices of the monks – the epitome of rugged, manly, muscular Christianity – all that standing in cold water, wearing hair shirts, endlessly genuflecting and living off a diet of bread and water. It is also there in the strong consciousness of the power of physical elements reflected in numerous prayers about the sea, mountains, storms, wind, rain and fire. Many of these prayers were couched in terms of fear and awe rather than a romantic attachment to nature. One of the earliest poems from Iona began 'Father, do not allow thunder and lightning, lest we be shattered by its fear and its fire.' Prayers of protection and encirclement, belonging to the so-called *lorica* and *caim* genres, were similarly infused with strong physical imagery, in part influenced by the psalms but also reflecting the reality of life at this time. Celtic Christians lived close to nature without most of the creature comforts that we take for granted. This gave them a respect for the physical environment, as well as a fear of it. It also forced them to live much more physical lives than we do – no washing machines or vacuum cleaners in the Irish monasteries and no cars, or even a bicycle, to take the monks on their missionary journeys and pilgrimages.

Their puritan perfectionism also made the monks express their faith and discipleship in a physical way. Prayer for them was something to be approached and engaged in with the body as much as with the mind. The rule of Ailbe was typical in stipulating a hundred genuflections at the beginning of the day and a further hundred at matins. Subsequently monks were expected to genuflect three times 'earnestly' every time they passed the altar rail. While two hundred genuflections were regarded as the norm, more were seen as indicating a superior witness. An anchorite in Clonard was particularly admired for genuflecting seven hundred times a day. When they were not genuflecting, monks were expected to prostrate themselves on the ground and otherwise subject their bodies to severe ascetic disciplines. The rule of Comgall prescribed three hundred prostrations every day and three at every canonical hour. It also recommended 'two hundred blows of the hand every Lent, it will be a help'. Monks were also encouraged to perform the cross vigil, extending their arms in the form of a cross for long periods while standing, kneeling or lying prostrate on the ground. Just how long is indicated in the well-known story that when a bird laid its eggs in one of the outstretched hands of Kevin of Glendalough, he maintained the cross vigil for three weeks to allow them to hatch out.

These highly physical forms of prayer and devotion seem excessively and even dangerously masochistic to our modern outlook. The Celtic saints seem to have set out deliberately to inflict physical punishment on themselves and avoid comfort in any form. Beccán mac Luigdech's poem about Columba points out that it was on 'stone slabs ... not on cushioned beds he bent to his complex prayers' and twice refers to him 'crucifying' his body. We are back here to the centrality of witness, seen in terms of martyrdom and conforming to the sufferings of Christ. There was also a deeper and more positive theology of the body underlying these practices. The body was seen as the vehicle through which one attained glory through life-transforming ascetic practices. Thomas O'Loughlin argues that the writings of both early Welsh and early Irish Christians provide an important counter to the tendency of later

Western Christianity, both Catholic and Protestant, to denigrate the physical and over-emphasize the mind over the body:

> Running through a number of texts is the awareness of the body as the focus of human existence, not subordinate to the mind in a tortuous relation of subjection and culpability, but thematized as the locus of penance, where penance itself is not self-inflicted mutilation but the reception of new life and the beginning of the transformation that leads to glory.
>
> (Davies 1999:24)

Physicality had another important dimension in the significance accorded to place and locality. Loyalty to tribe, king and monastery encouraged such attachments. Physical boundaries, often marked by the erection of wooden crosses and cross-marked stones, were important both in the case of tribal kingships, or *tuatha*, and of monasteries which were designated as sacred spaces. There was also a wider interest in the whole concept of sacred places. Around 688, while abbot of Iona, Adomnán wrote one of the first ever Christian treatises about holy places, *De Locis Sanctis*. A guide to the holy sites of Scripture, it began at the gates of Jerusalem on the fringe of heaven and finished with the gates of Hell just north of Sicily. Illustrated with drawings, it was based on eyewitness accounts by a Frankish bishop, Arculf, who had visited the Holy Land, Constantinople and Rome. On the way back from his travels he was wrecked off the west coast of Scotland and found his way to Iona where Adomnán interviewed him about his experiences and recorded them for posterity. As we shall see, Celtic monks were very ambivalent about holy places and certainly did not share the widespread later mediaeval idea that pilgrimage to holy sites and relics induced a special spiritual 'buzz'. But place was nonetheless important for them, not least in finding one's own place of resurrection or desert in a particularly inaccessible and inhospitable location.

In common with other early Christians, the Celtic monks of the golden age saw a clear link and overlap between the spiritual and the physical. What might be regarded as supernatural encounters and experiences, both with good and evil forces and spirits, often had a tangible physical dimension. This is well illustrated in Adomnán's account of Columba's day long encounter with a line of foul black devils armed with iron spikes and drawn up ready for battle (page 88). The lives of other saints contain similar encounters with supernatural spirits embodied in physical or at least quasi-physical form.

The physical landscape impinged on the spirituality and beliefs of Celtic monks in very different ways, both inducing fear of the elements, as in an early poem from Iona asking for God's protection from thunder and lightning, and inspiring the lyrical hermits' poems about the delights of living in a little hut close to a flowing stream and with the birds singing overhead, which have been much quoted to illustrate the 'green' credentials and closeness to nature of Celtic Christianity. It is now thought that these idealized nature poems were in fact written by monks in large urban monastic complexes in the ninth and tenth centuries and represent an early example of romantic Celtic Christian nostalgia, being sophisticated literary creations rather than actual expressions of closeness to nature. (See Bradley 1999:33-34).

In later mediaeval Celtic Christianity, there was much more explicit interest in another aspect of the inter-relationship between the physical landscape and the supernatural sphere with the identification of places which afforded access into the otherworld. St Patrick's Purgatory, a cave on one of the islands in Lough Derg in Donegal where Patrick was supposed to have been given access to the underworld, developed as a pilgrim site in the twelfth century. Other less well-publicized sites with similar supposed properties included Geata Ath nam Marbh, the Gate of the Ford of the Dead, on the south end of the island of Jura which was believed to provide a passage between this world and the afterlife and the legendary tunnel leading to hell at Clach-Tholl, a raised natural arch located at the end of the Appin peninsula in Argyll.

In a very different way, physical landscape and the spiritual power of perceived holy places have assumed increasing importance in the modern revival of Celtic Christianity with monastic sites like Iona, Glendalough and Lindisfarne becoming major pilgrim destinations.

6 PROVISIONAL

A strong sense of provisionality underlies both the writings and the practices of the Irish monks. It comes out both in their theology, such as it is, and in their approach to life and worship, not least in relation to church buildings.

Nowhere does this theme come out more clearly than in the sermons of Columbanus, who was born around 543 in Leinster, became a member of the monastic community at Bangor, and set out in 591 to journey across continental Europe, setting up monasteries along the way in what are now France, Switzerland and Italy, and eventually dying in Bobbio in 615.

Again and again, his sermons pointed to the transitory and fleeting nature of this life, its seductive and illusory quality, and the importance of regarding it simply as a road along which we must journey, without being distracted on the way, while keeping our eyes fixed on our destination and heavenly home. 'Our first duty is to love nothing here', he preached, 'but to love the things above'. This message was eloquently expounded in his fifth sermon:

> Human life, fragile and marked for death, how many have you deceived, beguiled and blinded? While in flight, you are nothing; while in sight, you are a shadow; while you rise up, you are but smoke. What are you then, human life? You are the wayfaring of mortals and not their living. You are the way that leads to life, but not life itself, for you are a true way, but not an open one: brief for some and long for others, broad for some and narrow for others, joyful for some and full of grief for others, but for each and every one, you hurry on and cannot be called back. A way is what you are, a way, but you are not evident to all. Though many see you, few understand that you are indeed a way… You are to be traversed and not inhabited: wretched human life. For a road is to be walked on and not lived in, so that they who walk upon it may dwell finally in the land that is their home.
>
> (Davies 1999:353-4)

Alongside this emphasis on the essentially provisional and transitory nature of life, the Irish monks adopted a similar approach to worship. It seems that when they celebrated communion, the bread and wine remaining at the end were consumed immediately and not kept in a special tabernacle or aumbry as a reserved sacrament. The monastic churches themselves were simple structures made of wood – they could easily be extended or knocked down as circumstances demanded. Other buildings in the monastic compound where the monks, lived, worked, ate and slept were usually constructed either out of wattle and daub or wood and had a similarly temporary and provisional feel and appearance. The early crosses erected around monastic sites and as grave markers were made of wood – stone crosses only started appearing some time after the 'golden age' in the ninth and tenth centuries.

This style of building, especially as applied to churches and places of worship, echoed the approach of the Ancient Israelites during their long wanderings through the wilderness when they worshipped a God who travelled with and before them, appearing in a pillar of cloud by day and a pillar of fire by night, His presence symbolized in a portable tabernacle or tent. In retrospect, they felt much closer to the Divine presence throughout this period of wandering than when they later settled in the promised land and built a massive stone temple to house the Holy of Holies. Certainly the prophets felt that the Israelites lost their fervour and faith when they stopped being wanderers and moved from this provisional approach to a much more settled and institutional one. The Lord himself preferred to be worshipped on the move rather than tied down to one place, judging by his words to Nathan the prophet when King David expressed his desire to build a permanent temple: 'Are you the one to build me a house to live in? I have not lived in a house since the day I brought up the people of Israel from Egypt to this day, but I have been moving about in a tent and a tabernacle' (2 Samuel 7:5-6).

The Irish monks, in common with the other early Celtic-speaking Christian inhabitants of the British Isles, had a similar outlook to the Israelite wanderers through the desert, preferring journeying and pilgrimage to settled existence and feeling that worship, like other activities in this world, was essentially provisional and that this quality should be expressed in the buildings in which it took place. Hence the lack of stone buildings in monasteries, even for churches, something that Bede commented on when he describes how unusual was Ninian's 'church of stone', *Candida Casa* or the White House at Whithorn. The Normans, like the Romans before them, took a diametrically opposite view, believing that religious rituals and worship should take place in massive temples of stone designed to last for centuries and expressing the values of solidarity, permanence, grandeur and splendour. For the Normans, God was properly to be worshipped and glorified in magnificent permanent buildings like Durham Cathedral. The indigenous Christians who preceded them had a very different approach that emphasized the provisionality of worship, the impermanence of all human constructs and the essential transitory and passing nature of this life and this world.

7 PATTERNED

I began the first chapter of *The Celtic Way* as follows:

> Perhaps the strongest and also the most elusive symbol of their faith which our Celtic Christian forebears have left us are those endlessly intertwining and interlacing ribbons and ever twisting spirals which adorn the faces of the high standing crosses and the pages of their illuminated manuscripts.

I went on to discuss some of the explanations for these patterns, their origins and possible meaning, and to suggest that they may have expressed a sense of encirclement and protection, themes found in so many Celtic prayers, holding at bay the powers of the darkness and chaos and keeping danger without. I continued:

> There is another theme which I find very powerfully expressed in these most characteristic features of Celtic Christian art. It is the principle of constant movement. The endlessly intertwining ribbons that make up the Celtic knot, like the swirling curves and spirals of the illuminated manuscripts, suggest a world and a faith which is in a state of perpetual motion. This is not the wildly chaotic and rather frenzied activity that so much modern abstract art seems to suggest. It is much more ordered and controlled with an intricate symmetry, a definite pattern and the constant sense of being circumscribed within clearly defined bounds. But the overwhelming sense is one of movement and progress with the lines travelling ever onwards, even if they are constantly doubling back on themselves, ducking under or crossing over each other and ultimately always coming back where they started.
>
> (Bradley 1993: 1)

Twenty-five years on, I continue to be fascinated and drawn in by the serpent and boss motifs on high standing crosses and the endlessly intertwining lines and swirling curves on the illustration pages of illuminated manuscripts. I stand by what I wrote then about the theme of patterning which seems so strong and central in the artwork produced in the Irish monasteries and their offshoots in Scotland, Wales and Northern England from the eighth to the eleventh centuries.

Many of these patterns belong to a wider Celtic culture. Similar swirling curves, spirals, knotwork and geometric designs with intertwining foliage, animals and birds characterize the artefacts found in the major excavations at La Tène and Hallstat. There are a number of striking features about this Celtic artwork. It is free and abstract with no attempt at realism or naturalism. It is not representational like the art of the Greeks and Romans with its concern for proper perspective. Rather it seems much more symbolic and metaphorical, designed to express mystery and, like icons in the Eastern Orthodox tradition, to draw those who view it into deeper contemplation and meditation.

There are significant innovations in the insular art of the Irish monasteries which are not found with the same emphasis or concentration in wider Celtic European culture. One such is the use of the diamond shaped lozenge design which is found so prominently in the *Book of Kells*. It is on Mary's right shoulder in the depiction of the Virgin child, at the intersection of the *Chi Rho* letters on the page illustrating the birth of Christ in Matthew's Gospel, at the centre of the page of symbols in St John's Gospel and on the cover of the book held by John in the portrait of the evangelist. In the *Book of Armagh* the concluding words of St John's Gospel are enclosed in a lozenge which occupies the central space on the last page. The lozenge shape also appears prominently on a number of high standing crosses, notably at Moone and at Kilbroney, County Down, where it is positioned at the centre of the cross-head. It is also found on the Tara and Cavan brooches and carved on the side of a doorway of an early monastic church at Fore, County Westmeath. Hilary Richardson and other art historians and archaeologists have persuasively argued that this lozenge symbol represents Christ as the Logos, or Word, as designated in the prologue to John's Gospel. It can, perhaps, be taken as evidence to back up the assertion made by Philip Newell and others that the fourth Gospel had a special place in the hearts and devotions of Celtic Christians. It is noticeable that in the

Book of Kells the diamond-shaped lozenge is always edged with purple and gold, the colours used to suggest imperial majesty. If it is pointing to the majesty and kingship of Christ, this particular piece of patterning again suggests icon-like symbolism, mystery and metaphor.

It was not just the artwork produced in the monastic workshops and scriptoria that is distinguished by its patterning, rhythm, movement and flowing circular character. So too was the life and the faith of the monks themselves. All monastic life is, of course, based on pattern and rhythm. There is the balance between prayer, physical labour and study or *lectio divina*. Monastic rules enable those who intentionally obey them to live divinely ordained and established patterns. In the words of Oliver Davies, 'the monastic vocation is primarily the choice of an evangelical way of life which will be lived out until death in the daily rhythms of the conversion of body, mind and soul to God' (Davies 1996: 67). It is about the sanctification and patterning of time. Irish monastic rules seem especially to have emphasized these qualities of rhythm and balance. A key influence here was undoubtedly the principle of curing by contraries pioneered by John Cassian, the monk credited with bringing the ideas and practices of Eastern desert monasticism to the early mediaeval west. The influence of this approach and the wider emphasis on balance was very clearly evident in the opening paragraph of the early seventh century *Alphabet of Devotion* attributed to Colmán, founder of the monastery of Llan Elo in County Offaly which spelled out what constitutes a holy life:

> Faith with action, desire with constancy, calmness with devotion, chastity with humility, fasting with moderation, poverty with generosity, silence with discussion, distribution with equality, endurance without grievance, abstinence with exposure, zeal without severity, gentleness with justice, confidence without neglect, fear without despair, poverty without pride, confession without excuse, teaching with practice, progress without slipping, lowliness towards the haughty, smoothness towards the rough, work without grumbling, simpleness with wisdom; humility without partiality.
>
> (Clancy & Márkus 1995: 200)

The lives of the Celtic saints described a similar rhythm and patterning of life with periods of intense involvement in the affairs of the monastery, and indeed the world beyond the monastic *vallum*, alternating with times of withdrawal from the world to be alone with God. Admonán's *Life of Columba* was typical in portraying the saint both as a Chief Executive Officer running a busy complex of monasteries, interacting with numerous people and immersing himself in political affairs and dynastic disputes, and as a lonely hermit who regularly retreated to the island of Hinba for solitary prayer and contemplation. Perhaps his two Gaelic nicknames, Crimthann, the fox, and Colm Cille, the dove of the church, testified to these two sides of his life and character – the wily, skilful administrator, negotiator and leader and the humble, gentle man of prayer. Many of the other Celtic saints were similarly portrayed as engaging both in practical good works and action and in contemplation and withdrawal from the world.

In living these balanced, rhythmic, patterned lives combining action and contemplation, community and isolation, engagement and withdrawal, they were of course following Jesus as he is portrayed in the Gospels – sometimes surrounded by crowds and deeply engaged with others, at other times alone walking by the lakeside or in the mountains. Eugene Peterson's *The Message* has Jesus say in Matthew 11, 'Walk with me and work with me – watch how I do it. Learn the unforced rhythms of grace'. (Peterson 1975:34). These unforced rhythms of grace, like the natural rhythms of breathing out and breathing in, were also emphasized by the nearest that we have to theologians and preachers in early mediaeval insular Christianity. Eurigena saw creation as a theophany of God, a continuous expression of procession and return with creation coming forth from God, almost as an emanation, and returning to God. Columbanus in his fifth sermon used language which seems to prefigure that of T.S. Eliot in *Four Quartets*: 'Every day you depart and every day you return; you depart in returning and you return in departing, different ending, same beginning.'

His words have a similarly elusive, circular quality to the endless intertwining spirals and knotwork on the high crosses and in the illuminated manuscripts. They speak, like the monastic vocation, of patterns, rhythm and balance and of movement and fluidity, not random and chaotic but ordered, circumscribed and lived out in conscious imitation of and witness to Christ, the Logos and the one who calls his disciples to learn the unforced rhythms of grace.

5
Attributes of God

1 PRIMORDIAL

> The High Creator, the Unbegotten, Ancient of Days,
> Was without origin of beginning, limitless,
> He is and will be for endless ages of ages.
>
> (Clancy & Márkus 1995:45)

The sonorous opening lines of the *Altus Prosator*, a somewhat forbidding poem attributed to Columba, paint a picture of God as primordial, foundational, utterly transcendent and awesome. A similar emphasis on divine mystery, distance and ineffability pervades many of the prayers and poems from the golden age of Celtic Christianity. Pelagius describes God as 'that eternal, ineffable majesty and incalculable power' (Rees 1991: 53). The preface to the Eucharistic liturgy in the Stowe Missal begins by speaking of God as all powerful and ever-living, one and immortal, incorruptible and unmoving, invisible and faithful, most high and magnificent (see O'Loughlin Journeys 2000: 69).

In technical theological terms, these early Celtic writings stand very much in the apophatic tradition which emphasizes the unknowability of God. Thomas O'Loughlin describes Eurigena as the western theologian who more than any other in the early Middle Ages emphasizes the unknowability of God. This idea was accompanied by the approach already noted as being similar to that adopted by Martin Buber that God is not so much to be expressed as experienced and addressed – in other words there is not much point in endless systematic theological speculation about the divine nature and being of God; rather God is simply to be approached directly through prayer and adoration.

This approach partly explains why so little systematic theology comes out of this period of the Christian history of the British Isles. It was seen as a fruitless speculative exercise, and one which in some ways reduced and analysed God's primordial and foundational character. This point is strongly made by Columbanus in his sermons where he constantly reminds his hearers that God is known not by words but by faith:

> Seek the supreme wisdom, not by verbal debate, but by the perfection of a good life, not with a tongue but with the faith which issues from singleness of heart, not with that which is gathered from the guess of a learned irreligion. If you seek the unutterable by discussion, He will fly farther from you than He was; if you seek by faith, wisdom shall stand in her accustomed station at the gate, and where she dwells she shall at least in part be seen. But then she is also truly in some measure attained, when the invisible is believed in a manner that passes understanding; for God must be believed invisible as He is, though He be partly seen by the pure heart.
>
> (Walker 1957: 65-7)

This prioritising of faith over reason, discussion and enquiry did not amount to an anti-intellectualism. Although there is much emphasis in the writings of Columbanus, Pelagius and Eurigena on the seductive dangers of abstract theological speculation and the fact that the supreme mystery of God can never be grasped by the human mind, they also commend reading and study, as long as it is focused on the Scriptures and interspersed with frequent prayer. Irish monasteries had comprehensive and well-stocked libraries and it is clear that monks were encouraged to spend time in *lectio divina* and to use their minds. Intellectual activity, whether on the part of monks or lay Christians, was, however, seen as subordinate to the all-important imperative of prayer and obedience to the awesome, all-powerful God. Pelagius counselled the 14-year-old Demetrias, 'your reading must be done in moderation and a limit imposed upon it by prudence and not by fatigue … intemperate enthusiasm for reading can come in for criticism' (Rees 1991:62).

The opening phrase of the *Altus Prosator*, with its emphasis on 'the High Creator', highlights two dominant attributes of God – his distant and regal majesty and his work of creation. Creation was widely viewed within Celtic Christianity as the prime work of God. There was also an emphasis on divine transcendence as well as on divine immanence. God was viewed as standing outside his creation. Eurigena emphasised the distinction between the Creator and his creatures in his *Peripyseon* although as we shall see below there is a distinct ambiguity in his writing on this subject. The preface of *Liber de Ordine Creaturarum* (The Book of the Order of Creation), a manual for training priests probably written in Ireland in the seventh century, which gives an orderly account of creation based on the opening chapters of Genesis, similarly distinguishes between Creator and creatures. The *Altus Prosator* devotes a considerable amount of attention to the subject of creation. There is also a good deal in it about the Fall and the second coming of Christ which is described in dramatic and apocalyptic terms. By contrast, there is almost nothing about redemption and salvation.

There is a story that attributes the *Altus Prosator* to Columba and suggests that Pope Gregory the Great read it and complained that it did not make enough of the theme of redemption and was too narrowly focused, almost in a Deist way, on God the Father and Creator at the expense of the two other persons of the Trinity, Jesus Christ and the Holy Spirit, whom he felt were hardly mentioned. Columba is said to have responded by writing the much more Christologically focused *In Te, Christe credentium miseraris omnium*, a two part hymn which described Christ both in terms of his significance to believers and his work for humanity. This has found its way into several modern hymnbooks in the translation which begins 'Christ is the World's Redeemer, the Lover of the Poor' set to the pulsating Irish tune 'Moville'.

Whether this story is true or not, and it is most probably apocryphal, it points to an undeniable emphasis in many early Celtic Christian sources on creation at the expense of redemption. Whether this amounts to a creation-centred theology is a moot point. It is combined with a very strong sense of sin and an attachment to the doctrine of the Fall which makes it very different indeed from the modern creation-centred theology of Matthew Fox and his disciples. It is perhaps best seen as an appreciation of the mighty works of God, conceived of in terms of an awesome and omnipotent primordial being. In so far as God can be known, and that is not really very much at all because he ultimately remains an ineffable mystery, it is perhaps through his work of creation. There are clear echoes here of Paul's Epistle to the Romans 1.19-20: 'Ever since the creation of the world God's invisible nature, namely his eternal power and deity, has been clearly perceived in the things that have been made'. For several of those writing in the golden age of Celtic Christianity creation pointed most clearly to the utter unknowability of God. This was certainly the message of Columbanus who pointed out in his first sermon that just as we cannot really penetrate and understand the wonders and mysteries of creation, even less can we understand the much more profound depth and mystery of the Creator:

> Seek no farther concerning God; for those who wish to know the great deep must first review the natural world ... If a man wishes to know the deepest ocean of divine understanding, let him first if he is able scan that visible sea, and the less he finds himself able to understand of those creatures which lurk beneath the waves, the more let him realize that he can know less of the depths of its Creator. The one God, the Trinity, is an ocean that cannot be crossed over or searched out. High is the heaven, broad the earth, deep the sea and long the ages; but higher and broader and deeper and longer is the knowledge of Him Who is not diminished by nature, Who created it of nought. Understand the creation, if you wish to know the Creator; if you will not know the former, be silent concerning the Creator ... For just as the depth of the sea is invisible to human sight, even so the Godhead of the Trinity is found to be unknowable by human senses.

> (Walker 1957 :65)

2 POWER

One word occurs again and again in connection with invocations and descriptions of the Father, the Son, the Holy Spirit and the Trinity as a whole in Celtic prayers, poems and sermons from the sixth to the eleventh century – God is conceived and spoken of first and foremost in terms of power. We need look no further than the opening lines of one of the best-known hymns from the golden age of Celtic Christianity, *St Patrick's Breastplate* (and here I use the translation by Noel Dermot O'Donoghue):

> For my shield this day I call
> A mighty power:
> The Holy Trinity!

> (Mackey 1989:46)

The poem goes on to use the word power in introducing all of its invocations of Christ's activities – his birth and baptism, crucifixion and burial, rising and ascending and descending and judgment – as well as in its reference to the love of the cherubim and seraphim. Indeed, the word power appears six times in the first ten lines of the Breastplate poem. Another prayer attributed to Patrick begins:

> May the strength of God pilot us.
> May the power of God preserve us.

Divine power also features very prominently in the *Altus Prosator* where it is first acknowledged in terms of God's creative activity:

> This great globe doth God the Highest
> By his power all surely keep.

The *Altus Prosator* goes on to portray power as the dominant characteristic of Christ in his Second Coming, which, as we have already noticed, is made much more of than either the Crucifixion or Resurrection in this poem (and here I use a versified nineteenth century translation):

> When from Heaven to Earth descending
> Comes the Christ in power divine,
> Then the Signal Cross, his banner,
> Shall all glorious shine.

Prominent early Celtic preachers and theologians also made much of divine power. Columbanus referred to God in one of his sermons as 'the all-powerful, invisible, unfathomable, ineffable and unsearchable'. Pelagius described God in his letter to Demetrias as 'that eternal, ineffable majesty and incalculable power'. As these quotations show, emphasis on God's power went alongside reference to his ineffable primordial quality and the two attributes are difficult to separate out. But the overall effect is impossible to escape – there is much more on divine omnipotence than on divine mercy, forgiveness or compassion. Thomas O'Loughlin has pointed out how strong the theme of omnipotence was in Patrick's understanding of God as 'the supreme actor whose power is unlimited, and constantly active…a stern Omnipotence who demands "every last penny".' Commenting on the tendency of modern enthusiasts for Celtic Christianity to emphasize the closeness and presence of God, O'Loughlin offers this salutary corrective:

We should remember that their sense of God was very often that of a mighty power hovering over every situation. The closeness is the overpowering closeness of the stern, all-seeing master. Prayers that begin 'All powerful, everlasting God' were said with awe and trembling, for his manifestations expressing his justice were at times all too close. But could a society which had been raided for slaves, had suffered a series of social disruptions and had lived with mayhem avoid this sense that there was a powerful force always circling around their lives and making itself felt in terrifying events?

(O'Loughlin 2000:34)

A striking feature of this emphasis on divine power is the use of royal language to depict both God and Jesus. Once again, we can turn to a much loved and still much sung early Irish hymn to illustrate this theme, the one that we know in translation as 'Be thou my vision'. It speaks of 'the high king of heaven'. The first verse of the original English translation made by Mary Byrne in 1905 begins:

Be thou my vision, O Lord of my heart,
None other is aught but the King of the seven heavens.

The versified translation made by Eleanor Hull in 1912 and still widely sung today speaks of divine power in both majestic and militaristic language:

Be Thou my battle Shield, Sword for the fight;
Be Thou my Dignity, Thou my Delight;
Thou my soul's Shelter, Thou my high Tower:
Raise Thou me heavenward, O power of my power.

High King of Heaven, my victory won,
May I reach Heaven's joys, O bright Heaven's Sun!
Heart of my own heart, whatever befall,
Still be my vision, O Ruler of All.

Several other early Irish poems and prayers similarly speak of God or Christ as *Ardrigh*, or High King. It should be pointed out that Celtic Christianity was not unique or unusual in this respect. Anglo-Saxon Christians similarly employed royal images and language when addressing God or Christ – Benedicta Ward's 1999 book on early English spirituality acknowledges this in its title *High King of Heaven*. Such usage was not surprising in a society based around the idea of kingship. It did not necessarily connotate remoteness, although it did undoubtedly suggest power and majesty. In the many kingdoms that made up the British Isles in this period, *tuaths* as they were known in the Irish speaking realms, rulers were often quite close to their subjects to whom they were related by family ties and bound by tribal loyalty and kinship.

The kingship of God and Christ was regarded as a broad, encompassing, benevolent rule which embraced peace, protection, justice as well as having more cosmic and metaphysical elements. God was worshipped as king of the elements – of sun and moon and the stars of the sky – king of grace and glory and generosity, as well as king of the angels and all the hierarchies of heaven in their order. The *Altus Prosator* portrays a very hierarchical heaven, with God presiding from its summit over a descending order of heavenly beings from the archangels, through the seraphims and cherubims to the angels, all of which he has created along with 'Principalities and Thrones, Powers and Virtues'. In early Irish texts Christ was similarly described as the king of victories and the king of Sunday (*Righ an Domhnaigh* in Irish). The emphasis here is very much on the more awesome and magisterial attributes of both the divine Father and Son and their distance from their creation. It is only very much later, for example in the late-nineteenth-century *Carmina Gadelica*, that we find references in Celtic language sources to Christ as king of the poor and king of tenderness as well as king of glory, king of grace and king of life.

A somewhat forbidding but inescapable aspect of this emphasis on divine power and kingship is the central role accorded to both God the Father and the Son as judges. The theme of judgement looms large in most of the early extant texts from insular Christianity. Dread of it permeates Patrick's *Confessio*: 'With all my heart I dread with fear and trembling this sentence on that day, which no one can evade or hide from, when every single one of us shall render an account of even the least sins before the judgement seat of the Lord Christ' (Davies 1999:68-9). God's judgement is graphically described in the *Altus Prosator*:

> At the Lord's tribunal trembling,
> For just judgment we shall stand;

For each act its own due motive-
For each word – He will demand:
Of all ill each word and action
Long concealed shall face the sight:
Books of conscience long in hiding
Shall lie open to the light.

The Last Judgement was a common subject for depiction on Irish high standing crosses, usually on their east faces. The Cross of Muiredach at Monasterboice depicts the blessed and the damned standing on either side of the figure of Christ in glory, with St Michael weighing souls below.

Hilary Richardson, an Irish academic and leading authority on the Irish high standing crosses, believes that they were essentially symbols of power and that their inspiration came from the cross of light seen in a vision by the Emperor Constantine on the eve of the Battle of the Milvian Bridge in 312. Inscribed on that cross was the message 'by this sign shalt thou conquer'. She argues that the Irish high crosses, like other early mediaeval crucifixes, were similarly seen first and foremost as signs of triumph and victory and notes that 'the Cross was not an allusion to Christ's passion: it was an expression of Divine Power' (Richardson 1984:128). This conforms with the portrayal of the Cross in the *Altus Prosator* where there is no mention of its suffering or shame, but it is rather described as Christ's 'signal standard and banner gloriously shining'. It is noticeable that Christ is more often depicted on Irish crosses as an infant with his mother or as the *Christus Victor* sitting enthroned in heaven than he is hanging suffering on the Cross of Calvary. Even when the Crucifixion is shown, Jesus is often clothed and not naked, emaciated and writhing in agony, as he is on later mediaeval crosses. Hilary Richardson suggests that the circle surrounding the cross arms which gives the Celtic cross its distinctive ringed appearance represented a halo, wreath or crown further emphasising the *Christus Victor* theme. It has also been suggested that the wheeled cross is an adaptation of the *ChiRho* monogram, formed from the first two letters of the name Christ in the Greek language, which was also the symbol that Constantine saw in the sky and ordered to be displayed on his soldiers' shields. The image of *Christus Victor* is also found on smaller artefacts such as the Athlone Crucifix.

Dominant themes in the lives of the Celtic Saints also relate to this underlying emphasis on divine power. The ubiquitous miracle stories that often raise modern eyebrows reflect the conviction that the saints manifested and transmitted God's power in their own mighty and miraculous works. Their biographers portray them charging around the country like Power Rangers, zapping their pagan foes and performing spectacular conjuring tricks to prove the superior power of Christianity. This is clearly evident in Adomnán's Life of Columba, which is largely a collection of what the author described as 'Miracles of Power'. These include the story of Columba's reaction when he found that the gates of the pagan king Brude's fortress were not opened to receive him. He signed them with the Cross whereupon 'the bars were thrust back and the doors opened of themselves with all speed'. Later, when he was saying vespers with his brethren close to the stronghold of the pagan king, wizards came close to try and silence the sound of Christian prayer, whereupon Columba's voice was lifted up in the air 'like some terrible thunder so that the king and his people were filled with unbearable fear'. Patrick was similarly portrayed as performing miracles of power, including causing the pagan wizard Lochru, a Druid who had insulted the Christian faith, to be lifted up in the sky and then fall back to earth, hitting his head on a rock. Samson's miracles of power included healing the sick, banishing devils and raising the dead to life. Fursey was similarly credited with numerous healing miracles in his lifetime, including raising from the dead the young son of a Frankish duke. According to the eighth-century *Miracula Ninie Episcopi*, among the countless good works performed by Ninian with the help of 'the almighty ruler and revered power of the world, the Lord of miracles' was one in which, discovering that there were no green vegetables available for the monks' dinner, he caused a prolific crop to grow to maturity within the space of a few hours from seeds planted in the monastic garden.

The clear message of these miracle stories is that the power of God is there to be accessed and channelled through and by the especially faithful. Many of them echo the Gospel accounts of Jesus' miracles – there are numerous descriptions of Celtic saints stilling storms and winds, healing the sick and casting out demons and Columba is even depicted as turning water into wine for a Eucharistic celebration. Such activities are clearly understood as manifestations of divine power through God's agents. The miracles performed by the Celtic saints are not the product of human activity but are rather both dependent on and manifestations of divine agency and intervention. As Tim Clarkson, a modern biographer of Columba, points out, they show God's limitless power 'manifested in the special human beings whom He has chosen for a Divine purpose' (Clarkson 2012:11). Adomnán makes both their source and purpose abundantly clear in his comments after describing Columba's encounter with the Loch Ness monster (the first known mention of Nessie) whom he miraculously stopped in its tracks by making the sign of the cross : 'Even the heathen natives who were present at the time were so moved by the greatness of the miracle they had witnessed that they too magnified the God of the Christians. The Almighty declared his glorious name in the sight of a heathen people through these miracles of power'. (Sharpe 1995: 176, 184)

In his interesting study of Columba's miracles, James Bruce has argued that they are to be taken as eschatological signs of the kingdom of God breaking through into this world. Adomnán, he maintains, presents Columba as one who brings the eschatological kingdom of God into partial realization. The saint's supernatural actions and attributes, which include miracles, prophecies and visions of heavenly light and angels, are true proofs of faith and the flowering of this faith manifests the kingdom. Here we are presented with a much wider and more theologically nuanced concept of divine kingship which goes beyond mere comparison with earthly human rules to encompass God's ultimate reign of righteousness and justice.

Did this emphasis on divine power and authority, with its very hierarchical view of heaven, have consequences for how Celtic Christians viewed the powers of this world? Were they inclined to favour those in authority and emphasize earthly hierarchies? This is a complex area. At one level, they were conscious of the transitory nature of human power. The *Altus Prosator* reflects that:

> The momentary glory of the kings of the present world,
> Fleeting and tyrannical, is cast down at God's whim.

Yet at another level, there is no doubt that there was considerable respect and support for human authority, including monarchical power, especially when it was exercised with justice, mercy and equity. Christianity and kingship came into the British Isles together replacing paganism and the arbitrary rule of tribal warlords and the new institutions of church and monarchy did much to support each other. It was a relationship which brought mutual benefits. The church gained land, endowment and protection from rulers who in their turn received the benefits of prayerful support and the legitimacy that came from Christian coronations. In my book on Columba, I pointed to his role as a king maker and pointed to his support for the institution of monarchy. Like most Celtic Christians, he was anything but egalitarian, ruling his own monastic family in a decidedly autocratic way and having a distinct penchant for kings and princes, that is when they were Christians rather than pagans. This adulation of earthly monarchs was inspired by a sense that they were modelling in their own rule the kingship of Christ and a realisation that they brought stability, protection of the weak and the rule of law to communities which had so recently been dominated by wild, marauding warlords and savage chieftains.

Outside charismatic circles with their emphasis on signs and wonders, this focus on miracles, monarchy and other manifestations of divine power is rather alien to many contemporary western Christians. We need to remind ourselves just how brutal and violent life was for most of those living in the early Middle Ages and how tangible and terrible they felt the power of evil to be. *St Patrick's Breastplate* begins its list of the ills from which God's protection was needed with 'dark powers that assail me', a reminder that bad forces were seen potentially as every bit as powerful, pervasive and present as good ones. This is why divine power, protection and presence were so important and valued and why the omnipotent God of Celtic Christianity was a very different kind of deity from the vulnerable, wounded, suffering God of much late twentieth and early twenty first century theology.

3 PROTECTION

A striking number of prayers in the early Celtic tradition are heartfelt calls for divine protection and deliverance from a host of dangers and evils which are often enumerated in precise and considerable detail. They include those in the so-called *lorica* or breastplate tradition, of which *St Patrick's Breastplate* is the best-known, and another distinctive group of *caim* or encircling and encompassing prayers.

The context for these prayers is the fragility and uncertainty of life in the early Middle Ages which has already been highlighted in the last section. Disease, pestilence, natural disasters and the violence endemic in a tribal society still dominated in many places by warlords conspired to make life for many people nasty, brutish and short. It is hardly surprising that in the face of such dangers and uncertainties God's protective powers should be so strongly emphasized and invoked. Father, Son and Holy Spirit, the Trinity as a whole, along with the Saints, the faithful and even on occasions the physical elements, were all enlisted as shields and defenders against misfortune, evil, and sudden death. Once again, the inspiration behind this was clearly biblical. St Paul's list in Ephesians 6.14-16 of the protective armour available to Christians - specifically the breastplate of righteousness, the shield of faith, the helmet of salvation and the sword of the Spirit - inspired a whole genre of Irish prayers and poems.

St Patrick's Breastplate classically expresses the approach of this *lorica* tradition, invoking the protective power of God and the presence of Christ to ward off danger from a host of potential evils and threats, including poison and burning, drowning and wounding, false prophesyings, pagan devisings, heretical lying, unlawful knowledge and spells cast by women, blacksmiths and Druids. It is one of many similar prayers written in Irish between the ninth and eleventh centuries. What is particularly striking and unusual about *St Patrick's Breastplate* is that as well as calling on God and Christ, it also invokes the physical elements, including the virtues of the star-lit heaven, the sun's life-giving ray, the whiteness of the moon at evening, the flashing of the lightning, the whirling wind, the stable earth and the deep salt sea. These intriguing and unusual additions to the usual range of protective forces marshalled in the *lorica* could suggest a hangover from pre-Christian Celtic worship of the physical elements or a pantheistic view, maybe even a touch of the emanationist theology associated with Eurigena (see page 84). In fact, the physical elements were as likely to appear in the list of dangers from which protection was being sought in the *lorica* as to be invoked as protectors. The *Noli Pater* prayer attributed to Columba beseeched God not to allow thunder and lightning, 'lest we be shattered by its fear and fire' and there are several other prayers which cast the forces of nature in similar negative terms.

The Breastplate prayers were often explicitly Trinitarian in their language about God. A good example is a ninth-century Irish poem which began: 'God be with me against all trouble, noble Trinity which is one, Father, Son, and Holy Spirit' and continued:

> The bright holy King of the sun, who is more beautiful than anything to which we have a right, is a wondrous refuge for me against the host of black demons.

> The Father, the Son, the glorious Holy Spirit, may these three protect me against all plague-bearing clouds.

The list of evils from which protection was sought in this poem included violent or sudden death, brigands' plundering, thunder and fire, weapons, dread and 'the bitterness of the winds'. It was not just the Trinity which was enlisted for its protective power but also a plethora of other human agencies, including 'every good saint who suffered on the earth below, every pious disciple who believed in Christ, everyone meek, everyone quiet, everyone sincere, everyone unsullied, every confessor, every soldier who exists beneath the sun ... every glorious pilgrim ... and every destitute person'. There is a clear expression here both of the doctrine of the Communion of Saints and also of the protective power of all faithful and good people everywhere – the combined company of the Church Militant and the Church Triumphant. The poem ended by coming back to God, or perhaps Christ, seen in his royal role: 'May my King guard me; may he aid me always; may I be at every need beneath the protection of God's hand.' (Murphy 1956:22-27)

Christ's cross was often invoked as a protective talisman and device. The author of an Irish prayer, thought to date from the tenth century and possibly to have come from a monastery with a connection to Columba, figuratively drew Christ's cross over specified parts of his body, including the lower belly, thighs and legs as well as the more usual head and face – there was even a special mention of 'Christ's cross over my teeth lest injury or harm come to me'. The protective power of the cross was also extended in this prayer over 'my community, my church' and in the next world but it was harnessed first and foremost as a personal aid: 'From the top of my head to the nail of my foot, O Christ, against every danger I trust in the protection of thy cross'. A Welsh poem found in the *Book of Taliesin* and headed 'Alexander's Breastplate' called on the protective power of the cross in a more general way:

> Christ's cross is bright,
> A shining breastplate
> Against all harm
> And all our enemies,
> May it be strong:
> The place of my protection.

The physical act of making the sign of the cross was seen as a way of averting danger and repelling evil. As already noted, Columba used it to spectacular and swift effect on the Loch Ness monster, thereby neutralising its power and stopping it in its tracks, on his journey through the Great Glen. He also used it to open the barred gates of the pagan Pictish king Brude's palace and to banish a devil from a milk pail.

Another physical expression of this theme of protection is to be found in the so-called *caim* or encircling prayers in which a circle was described, usually with the forefinger of the right hand, around an individual, a family, a home or even a community while at the same time God's protection was invoked to keep all evil from entering within its bounds. It has to be said that such prayers are found much more often in much later Gaelic sources, like the *Carmina Gadelica*, than in the earlier predominantly monastic material which has survived from the golden age of Celtic Christianity. A much quoted example comes from the pen of Alisdair Maclean, an early-twentieth-century Highland Church of Scotland minister:

> The sacred Three
> My fortress be,
> Encircling me.
> Come and be round
> My hearth and my home.

(Bradley 1993:47)

David Adam, the late-twentieth-century Vicar of Lindisfarne, has written several fine *caim* or encircling prayers, such as the one that begins 'Circle me Lord, keep protection near and danger afar'.

It is probably fair to say that this particular genre of protective prayers is predominantly a relatively modern phenomenon although the *caim* tradition does have earlier antecedents. Another rather earlier development, found certainly from the eleventh and twelfth centuries if not before, was the enlisting of the Celtic saints themselves as protectors and patrons and their invocation in prayers alongside the Trinity and the Virgin Mary. We see the full flowering of this development in the *Carmina Gadelica* in its many incantations invoking the aid of Columba, Patrick, Bridget and other Celtic saints in company with Jesus, Peter, Paul and Mary.

Alongside the prayers and the practice of signing the cross, there were other more physical aspects to this overarching theme of protection. Monasteries were seen as safe houses and spaces, often resorted to by those fleeing violence or persecution. Within the monastic *vallum* the values of God's kingdom rather than those of the human world prevailed – this meant that monasteries also became sanctuaries for criminals seeking forgiveness who were given the medicine of penance. The crosses which were erected around the boundaries of monasteries and churches designated areas of protection and safety as well as sanctity, as an early Irish rule laid down: 'Let the boundary of a holy place have signs around it. Wherever you find the sign of the cross of Christ, you will do no harm'. (Clancy & Márkus 1995:21).

The high standing crosses may also have acted as protectors against evil forces. This is certainly the view of the Celtic scholar Robin Flower. He sees them as having a semi-magical role as stone defences against evil in much the same way that old pre-Christian standing stones had been. Whether there was, in fact, any carry-over of pagan ideas in the purposes for which the high crosses were constructed, there was a clear biblical inspiration in their embodiment of the theme of protection. The most popular Scriptural scenes depicted on their shafts were those in which individuals facing perilous situations sought deliverance from God – Isaac about to be sacrificed by Abraham, David facing Goliath, Daniel in the lion's den and Shadrach, Meshach, and Abednego being tested in the fiery furnace. These scenes appear again and again, underlining the urgent concern with finding deliverance from danger which led to such a focus on the protective power of God in Celtic Christianity.

4 PRESENCE

If God was envisaged by the indigenous insular Christians of the British Isles in the early Middle Ages as primordial, transcendent, awesome and all-powerful, He was also conceived of as being intensely present both throughout creation and also through the spirit realms which were seen as being very near and close.

The intensity and ubiquity of this sense of presence is perhaps what modern writers have emphasized most when seeking to characterize Celtic Christianity. Among the first to point to it was the Scottish theologian John Macquarrie in his 1972 book *Paths in Spirituality*:

> At the very centre of this type of spirituality was an intense sense of presence. The Celt was very much a God-intoxicated man whose life was embraced on all sides by the divine Being. But this presence was always mediated through some finite this-world reality, say that it will be difficult to imagine a spirituality more down-to-earth than this one.
>
> (Macquarrie 1972:123)

James Mackey wrote in similar terms in the preface to his 1989 *Introduction to Celtic Christianity*:

> The nearness, the ubiquitous *presence* of the spiritual in all things and at all times ... is a powerful, permanent and characteristic Celtic conviction. In the end it may prove to be the most important contribution which the Celtic mind can still offer to the modern world.
>
> (Mackey 1989: 10-11)

For Oliver Davies, 'God was present to Christians from Celtic cultures in images and signs, in poetry and art, in sacrament and liturgy'. (Davies 1999:3). Donald Allchin, reflecting on the use of the Welsh word *presen*, derived from the Latin word *presentia*, meaning presence, as a synonym for the world in the Welsh poem written in the margin of a ninth century manuscript of Juvencus' Latin metrical version of the Gospels, noted that for Celtic Christians 'The world is the place of God's presence. God's presence makes the world at every moment.' (Allchin 1997:11)

There is no doubt that the early Celtic Christian sources express a strong sense of God's presence in and through his creation. As we have already observed, there was a marked emphasis on God's work as creator and with this came an understanding that God's works proclaimed his presence. This is clear from an affirmation of faith which, according to Bishop Tírechán, Patrick made when he was asked about the Christian God by one of the daughters of Lóegaire, the pagan high king of Tara:

> Our God is the God of all men, the God of heaven and earth, sea and rivers, of sun and moon and all the stars, of high mountains and lowly valleys, the God above heaven, the God in heaven, the God under heaven. He has his dwelling in heaven and earth and sea and in all that in them is. He inspires all things, He quickens all things, He is over all things, He supports all things. He makes the light of the sun to shine, He surrounds the moon and stars, has made wells in the arid earth, has placed dry islands in the sea and set stars to minister to the greater lights.

Several modern writers about Celtic Christianity have argued that the extent to which God was seen as being present in the natural and physical features of creation amounted to a kind of pantheism and suggested a syncretistic take-over of pagan Celtic worship of trees, rivers, and other natural physical features. Macquarrie, following his statement quoted above, went on to comment: 'The sense of God's immanence in his creation was so strong in Celtic spirituality as to amount sometimes almost to a pantheism. Of course Celtic Christianity was continuous with the earlier Celtic paganism.' (Macquarrie 1972:123). In fact, the early insular sources give no hint of anything approaching pantheism, understood as the belief that nature is identical with divinity and that everything composes an all-encompassing, immanent God. There is nothing remotely like the pre-Christian poem attributed to Amergin Glúrignel and entitled 'The Song of Amergin' which begins 'I am the wind on the sea; I am the ocean wave'. It is unfortunate and misleading that this poem sometimes appears in Celtic Christianity anthologies. As we have seen, there was a clear separation in early Celtic Christian writings between the Creator and his creation. The preface to the seventh-century *Liber de Ordine Creaturarum* is clear that 'Everything that is within our minds ought to be seen to admit one major distinction: between focusing on God and things; or put another way, we can distinguish between Creator and creatures'. (O'Loughlin Journeys 2000:73-4).

However, although there was a clear insistence on God's distance and separation from creation, there was also an undoubted sense of his presence throughout it. Divine transcendence and immanence were held together in a way that might seem paradoxical or even contradictory. We see these two seemingly incompatible divine attributes being equally affirmed in Columbanus' comment that 'while being present to everyone everywhere, God remains invisible'. It may be that what was in play here was something more akin to the concept of panentheism, understood as suggesting that God is in everything as well as having his own independent existence as creator. Eurigena, the nearest that Celtic Christianity came to producing a theologian, wrestled more than anyone with the paradox of divine transcendence and immanence and sought to hold on to both aspects of God. While at times maintaining emphatically the total separation of Creator and creatures, he also came near to espousing an almost pantheistic position, writing in *Periphyseon*: 'God is all things everywhere, and wholly in the whole, the Maker and the made, and the Seer and the seen....He is everything that truly is' (O'Meara 1988:111).

Eurigena has often been associated with espousing a doctrine of emanationism, by which is understood the idea that God did not create *ex nihilo*, or out of nothing, as orthodox Christian teaching would have it, but rather out of his own essence. The world is thus an emanation of or from God as well as being a theophany, or visible showing of him. It has come out of his being to which it will eventually return. This theory, which was condemned by the Pope in 1225, causing several of Eurigena's books to be put on the Index of forbidden writings, was expounded most fully in his *Periphyseon* which certainly comes close to panentheistic if not even pantheistic language:

> God and the creature are not two things distinct from one
> another; but one and the same. For both the creature, by
> subsisting, is in God; and God, by manifesting himself, in
> a marvellous and ineffable manner, creates himself in the
> creature, the invisible making himself visible, and the
> incomprehensible comprehensible, and the hidden revealed
> … the Creator of all things created in all things, and the

Maker of all things made in all things, and eternal he begins
to be, and immobile he moves into all things, and becomes
in all things all things.

(O'Meara 1988:112)

The dense and deep musings of this ninth-century philosopher-
theologian cannot necessarily be taken as indicative of the approach
of Celtic Christianity as a whole to the subject of divine presence.
There is nothing in the sources from its so-called golden age which
comes anywhere near Eurigena's espousal of emanationist and
panentheistic ideas. There was certainly a widespread belief,
springing perhaps in large part from immersion in the Psalms,
that in so far as God was to be known and encountered at all, it was
largely through his creation. An early Irish commentary on Psalm
19 noted that 'the elements sound and show forth the knowledge of
God'. This, however, was a very different matter from suggesting,
as Eurigena did, that God had entered completely and put himself
into all things. In his book *Celtic Fire* Robert Van de Weyer quotes
a catechism attributed to Ninian of Whithorn stating that the
fruit of all study should be 'to perceive the eternal word of God
reflected in every plant and insect, every bird and animal and every
man and woman' (Van de Weyer 1990:96). I have been unable to
verify this quotation. Nor can I identify or corroborate statements
attributed to Pelagius by both Van de Weyer and Philip Newell
in his book *Listening for the Heartbeat of God* to the effect that God's
spirit is present within all creatures and all plants (Newell 1997:11).
This panentheistic notion that God is to be found in every single
created thing is much more clearly found in the material collected
by Alexander Carmichael in the Highlands and islands of Scotland
in the late nineteenth century, notably the much quoted poem
which begins 'There is no plant in the ground but is full of his
virtue' (quoted Bradley 1993:58-59). There is nothing that I can
find expressing quite these sentiments in Celtic prayers or poems
written between the seventh and eleventh centuries.

If a slight note of caution perhaps needs to be sounded in
respect of the extent and nature of God's immanence in Celtic
Christian understanding, we can be less hesitant about affirming
its strong sense of the ubiquitous presence of Christ, surrounding
and encompassing each person. It is brought out very clearly in the

well-known verse in *St Patrick's Breastplate* which specifically invokes Christ's protective power:

> Christ be with me, Christ within me,
> Christ behind me, Christ before me,
> Christ beside me, Christ to win me,
> Christ to comfort and restore me.
> Christ beneath me, Christ above me,
> Christ in quiet, Christ in danger,
> Christ in hearts of all that love me,
> Christ in mouth of friend and stranger.

In much later popular Celtic spirituality, this sense of the closeness of Christ's presence is taken further and in a much more intimate direction. Carmichael's *Carmina Gadelica* contains several poems, prayers and incantations in which Jesus, often together with Mary, Michael, Brigit and the apostles Peter, Paul and John, are invoked and envisaged not just as close presences but as companions, sitting in a boat or lying down to sleep next to the one who is praying. This level of familiar intimacy is not found in the earlier sources but there is undoubtedly a strong sense in them of Christ's close, comforting and encompassing presence.

The presence of the Holy Spirit is also clearly apparent in the early Celtic Christian sources. The saints' lives are full of manifestations of the gifts of the Spirit as enumerated by Paul in 1 Corinthians 12, notably miracles, healing and prophecy, although not speaking in tongues. On a broader level, there is widespread acknowledgement of the presence and closeness of what might be described as the spiritual realm, often manifested in physical form. There is, in fact, no hard and fast divide between the spiritual and the material. Here Eurigena with his strong attack in *De Divisione Naturae* on any kind of dualism or division between the spiritual and the material does seem to articulate a theme which is found across Celtic Christianity. Spiritual and supernatural presences were enormously important in the lives of the saints and in the prayers and liturgies composed in monasteries. It is no wonder that several modern writers have followed John Macquarrie and others in using the term 'Celtic spirituality' in preference to 'Celtic Christianity'. The spiritual realm of angels, archangels and heavenly hosts, and indeed of devils and demons, was as real and as tangible to Celtic Christians as the physical world. James Mackey has identified the extent to which this panoply of spiritual presences had their own integrity and individuality as well as being part of the wider divine presence:

> This pervasive sense of spiritual presence ... is always ultimately the presence of the divine. But we should not let residual memories of arid theological disputes as to whether, for instance, 'spirit' in some religious literature is a person or an 'impersonal power', tempt us to try to divide and so constrict the richness of the material. When the spiritual powers present are depicted as persons, they are meant to be thought of as persons, not as ciphers for God's presence. They have their own efficacy, though they have it only by God's will and grace to them ... . The choirs of angels are as real as the sun and moon, and their power is invoked directly: they are not invoked as mere transmitters of prayers to God ... . The Celtic Christian at prayer was consciously a member of a great company that stretched from the persons of the Trinity through the powerful Angelic throngs to the least of the spiritual persons, the risen saints.
>
> (Mackey 1989:12)

Columba provides a particularly striking example of a Celtic saint who is unusually open to supernatural experiences and spiritual presences, although he is by no means the only one. Adomnán noted 'how great and special were his experiences of angelic visits and heavenly lights'. Those around him regularly saw the saint surrounded by hovering angels or a halo of bright light. A monk who spied on Columba as he stood praying with his arms stretched out on a small grassy knoll near the machar on the west shore of Iona (subsequently known as *Cnoc nan Aingeal*, or the Hill of the Angels) was amazed by what he saw:

> Holy angels, the citizens of the heavenly kingdom, were flying down with amazing speed, dressed in white robes, and began to gather round the holy man. After they had conversed a little while with St Columba, the heavenly crowd – as though they could feel that they were being spied on – quickly returned to the heights of heaven.
>
> (Sharpe 1995: 218)

Further stories in Adomnán's life describe a strange angelic light shining both on and from Columba when he was in church and a brilliant heavenly light filling the hut in which he remained for three days and nights on the island of Hinba communing with the Holy Spirit – the rays of this light could be seen at night, escaping through the chinks of the doors and through the keyholes. Adomnán also provided several accounts of the saint's encounters with both malevolent and benevolent spiritual presences. Perhaps the most dramatic example was the description of Columba praying alone on a wild corner of Iona and seeing 'a line of foul, black devils armed with iron spikes and drawn up ready for battle' flying across the sky and ready to attack his monastery. He flung himself into conflict with them until 'the angels of God came to his aid' and drove the devils off the island. Angels were also much to the fore at the end of Columba's earthly life. His servant Diarmaid, following the dying saint into the monastic church on Iona, saw the whole building filled with angelic light around the saint. At the moment of the saint's passing an elderly monk named Lugaid saw troops of angels coming down from heaven to bear his holy soul upwards.

The close presence of angels is also mentioned in several of the poems and prayers attributed to Columba, notably the one quoted at the end of this book which begins 'The path I walk, Christ walks it' and which contains the line 'Bright angels walk with me – dear presence in every dealing'. This sense of the close proximity and companionship of angels has remained a striking feature of Celtic prayers and poems into relatively modern times. A popular Irish bedtime prayer, probably dating from the nineteenth century and with many variations, began: 'Four posts around my bed, Four angels around my head, One to watch and one to pray, And two to keep the Devil away'. A poem by Patrick Kavanagh, who lived from 1905 to 1967, included the observation that 'among your earthiest words the angels stray'. George MacLeod (1895-1951) wrote in one of his prayers: 'Turn but a stone and an angel moves'.

Such tangible encounters with supernatural beings are not, of course, peculiar to Celtic Christianity. They are documented throughout the early and mediaeval church and are also a feature of contemporary charismatic Christianity. There does, however, seem to have been a particularly strong angelology reflected in the lives of the sixth and seventh-century Celtic saints and in Irish spiritual writings. Some modern exponents of Celtic Christianity have seen its enthusiasm for spiritual presences as a hangover from pagan beliefs and pre-Christian Celtic mythology with its strongly developed sense of the underworld and of supernatural beings. In this reading, angels took the place of fairies. Several commentators have portrayed Columba essentially as a druid-like seer, displaying the gifts of second sight and the sixth sense, and as much a pagan as a Christian figure in his prophecies and encounters with the supernatural. But in fact the inspiration for them as they are recorded by Adomnán and in other early sources is very clearly and exclusively Biblical. We do not need to look beyond the highly developed angelology of the Old and New Testaments, the Gospel accounts of Jesus' miracles and St Paul's writings about the gifts of the Spirit and the reality of spiritual powers, both good and evil, to find the source and inspiration for the numerous allusions to supernatural encounters and spiritual presences found in the literature that came out of the monasteries of early mediaeval Ireland, Scotland and Wales.

Among the most significant Biblical texts for early indigenous Christians in the British Isles in this regard was the opening verse of Hebrews 12 which begins 'Seeing we are surrounded by so great a cloud of witnesses'. There was in Celtic Christianity a very clear appreciation of the doctrine of the communion of saints, the union of the Church Militant on earth with the Church Triumphant in heaven and the closeness of the cloud of witnesses made up of those who had departed this life. A very narrow line separated the living and the dead who were seen as continuing spiritual presences in the world. It was not unknown for a monk to choose for his soul friend someone who had died and departed saints were regularly invoked for their continuing protective and healing powers beyond death. The heavenly host, made up both of departed saints and the various orders of cherubim and seraphim, angels and archangels, often identified and named, was seen as a hugely important and almost tangible presence, available to be called on for protection and help, and also engaged in ceaseless worship of the Trinitarian God in which activity it was united with Christians on earth. The preface to the *Stowe Missal* prays that the voices of the faithful may be joined with and admitted to the heavenly chorus made up of angels, dominations, seraphim and other powers. An illustration in the *Book of Kells* depicts Christ sitting on top of the temple at

Jerusalem forming the head of the body of the church while above him hover angels and archangels.

Another striking aspect of this emphasis on metaphysical and supernatural presences within the Celtic Christian tradition was an appreciation of dreams and visions as vehicles through which God communicates with his human creatures. Once again, of course, this is a very Biblical concept, as the stories about Jacob's ladder and Joseph's dreams and many others in similar vein testify. Dreams were critical in the lives of several Celtic saints. It was in a dream that Patrick was shown how to escape his teenage slavery in Ireland and a later dream called him back to walk and work among the Irish. Samson had a dream in which he was made a bishop, something which indeed later happened. Ita had a dream which an angel helped her to interpret. Visions played a central role in the life of Columba and Fursey, the Irish monk who went as an evangelist to East Anglia, became best known for his vivid visions of the afterlife (page 111).

There is a final aspect of the theme of presence which is worth mentioning here, although I will be taking it up in more detail in Chapter 7. Celtic Christianity was characterized by what could I think be described (though not by Christians in the British Isles from the seventh to eleventh centuries who very sensibly eschewed such jargon) as an ecclesiology of presence. I have argued elsewhere that presence might be a much better word than mission to encapsulate the heart of Columba's understanding of the role and purpose of the church (Bradley 1996: 81). The Irish monasteries practised first and foremost a ministry of presence rather than of evangelism, or perhaps we should call it evangelism understood through presence rather than proselytizing. Monks did go out preaching the good news of Jesus' kingdom and baptizing converts, but they spent more of their time witnessing to Christ within the bounds of their monasteries, praying, meditating, reading, receiving and counselling troubled penitents and pilgrims, offering hospitality and healing to guests – in other words, being present.

5 PLEROMA

The word pleroma is not one that I have found in any of the early monastic sources but it expresses a key theme in the Celtic Christian understanding of God – a sense of the fullness and abundance of God's creation and specifically of the spiritual and physical as the divine abode.

The concept of the pleroma or plenitude of God's creation is expressed particularly powerfully in the Psalms with their assertion that 'The earth is the Lord's and the fullness thereof' (Psalm 24.1) and their proclamation that every part of creation has a significance and importance to God in its own right, and not just for its usefulness to human beings:

> The trees of the Lord are watered abundantly,
> The cedars of Lebanon which he planted.
> In them the birds build their nests;
> The stork has her home in the fir trees.
> The high mountains are for the wild goat;
> The rocks are a refuge for the badgers.
>
> (Psalm 104.16-17)

Although the emphasis in the Hebrew Bible switches progressively from the universal to the particular, it does not portray a world made up of a collection of autonomous, independent individual entities. Rather it suggests a rich and varied creation united in interdependence and mutuality. Creation is portrayed as being especially brought together in praising its maker with whom there is a wonderful reciprocal relationship. The Psalms are full of images of diverse creatures responding to the lure and love of their creator, with birds and animals lifting their voices in song, rivers and streams gurgling their joy, the trees of the field clapping their hands and mountains and hills skipping forth like goats.

Given the huge influence of the Psalms on the insular Christian communities of the British Isles in the early mediaeval period, and especially on those living and working in the monasteries, it is not surprising to find these themes echoed prominently in their art, poetry and prayers. It is noticeable how often birds and animals feature in both the pages of illuminated manuscripts and the decoration of high crosses. Crammed into the postage stamp sized lozenge which stands at the intersection of the letters *Chi* and *Rho* on the page of the *Book of Kells* illustrating Christ's birth as recorded in Matthew 1.18 are four human figures, four animals and twelve birds. Lower down the same page are depictions of a cat playing with its kittens, an otter catching fish, and two moths and two mice nibbling at the host. Creatures appearing on other illustrated pages in the *Book of Kells* include sea serpents, hens, horses and various different kinds of dog. Among the species portrayed on the panels of Irish high standing crosses are ravens, doves, wrens, frogs, lions, deer, cats and sheep as well as the ubiquitous serpents and snakes. St Martin's Cross on Iona is one of several with carvings of birds, animals and plants on one face and Bible scenes on the other. Early Irish poems express a similar sense of a rich, diverse natural world embodying the pleroma and fullness of its creator. The Welsh poem scribbled in the margin of a ninth-century manuscript of Juvencus' metrical version of the Gospel begins with an echo of Isaiah 55.12:

> Almighty Creator, who hast made all things,
> The world cannot express all thy glories,
> Even though the grass and the trees should sing.

The doctrine of pleroma was classically expounded by Thomas Aquinas in his *Summa Theologiae* (1265-74) when he wrote that 'Distinction and variety in the world is intended by the first cause. God brings things into existence in order that His goodness may be communicated and manifested. One solitary creature would not suffice ... the whole universe together participates in the divine goodness more perfectly and represents it better than any single creature.' (Gilby 1955:85) This sense of the rich diversity of creation deliberately patterned by God and participating in the divine goodness is clearly anticipated in both the literature and art of the monastic communities in the early mediaeval British Isles. The themes of presence, praise and pleroma are interwoven, not least by the frequent recourse to images from the natural world, be they birds, beasts or plants. In the introduction to his anthology *Celtic Spirituality* Oliver Davies points out that 'Particularly in vernacular sources, nature appears as a theme to an unusual degree, and enjoys its own autonomy, rather than purely serving the human ends of atmosphere and mood' (Davies 1999:11)

As with so much else, the theme of pleroma and delight in the variety of nature became much more pronounced in later Celtic mediaeval sources. A twelfth-century Welsh poem included in Kenneth Jackson's anthology of Celtic nature poetry catalogues the tops of numerous plants, including ash trees, willows, gorse, reeds, broom, apple trees, rushes, heather and bracken, as 'delightful'. There is however a sting in the tale, with a reminder that plants wither and that their leaves prickle and will eventually fall. (Jackson 1995:64-8)

The early Celtic Christian understanding of pleroma went beyond the natural world to take in cosmological elements as well. God was expressed and found in the operation of the sun, the moon and the stars. Irish monks were interested in astronomy. Columba was portrayed by his near contemporary Dallan Forgaill as a stargazer, one who studied the sun, stars and moon and saw them in allegorical terms as pointing to the truths of the Bible and illuminating the mystery of God. The *Altus Prosator* proclaimed that when Christ descends from heaven in his second coming, 'the stars will fall to earth like the fruit of a fig tree'. The language is apocalyptic and eschatological, as with many of the early prayers, but it also conveys a sense of the whole of creation in its rich fullness and diversity participating in the outworking of the great Christian drama.

As one might expect from what we have already observed, a distinctly hierarchical approach was adopted to the notion of the pleroma, seen in terms of a rich and diverse order of both earthly and heavenly beings. The seventh-century *Liber de Ordine Creaturarum* set out a descending pattern of fifteen orders of creation, starting with spiritual creatures, 'the ordered ranks of the angels which form a hierarchy of spheres', followed by the upper heavens, the firmament and the waters above them, the sun, moon and sky, and then descending through the lower regions – the area of the earth's atmosphere between heaven and earth where 'devils and demons wander for the ruin of souls' to water and ocean, Adam's paradise, the terrestrial world and human life and down finally to the eternal fires of Hell. At the end of the list, standing outside this descending scale, is the future life (see O'Loughlin Journeys 2000:72-3).

The overall impression given here and in other early Celtic Christian texts is of a world which is patterned, layered, ordered, hierarchical, immensely rich and varied and where the spiritual and the physical are closely linked as well. Often expressed in apocalyptic and rather forbidding language, they address a God who is distinct from creation yet also intimately involved with it and whose power is shown forth and expressed throughout its rich pleroma, whether it be through the warmth and brilliance of the sun, the singing of angels and archangels or the playfulness of a cat chasing mice or an otter catching fish. It is the elemental perspective of a people living close to nature, somewhat in awe of its raw power but also immensely enthralled by all its wonderful variety and rich diversity.

6
Appropriate Human Responses

1 PENITENCE

An attitude of genuine and heartfelt penitence pervades the writings of the Celtic saints. While their hagiographers portrayed them as superhuman and ultra-holy wonder workers, the saints described themselves in very different terms. Patrick began his autobiographical *Confessio*: 'My name is Patrick. I am a sinner, a simple country person, and the least of all believers. I am looked down upon by many'. In similar vein, the author of the poem, *Adiutor Laboratorium*, attributed to Columba, described himself as 'a little man, trembling and most wretched, rowing through the infinite storm of this age'.

Underlying such statements was not a grovelling, masochistic self-flagellation, although it can sometimes seem like that, but a profound and very personal conviction of the human state of sin and alienation and a deep and heart-felt sense of contrition, remorse and humility leading to a constant state of self-examination and repentance and throwing oneself on the mercy of God. In the words of Hugh Connolly, an Irish priest who has written about the Irish Penitentials: 'The Celtic Christian started from a keen awareness of his capacity for sin. His humility was not some exaggerated form of self-abasement, but rather stemmed from a consciousness of what it means to be human, to be in need'. (Connolly 1995: 201). This penitential attitude was felt and expressed communally as well as individually – the earliest extant Irish litanies, which date back to the ninth century, and were gathered together by Charles Plummer in his *Irish Litanies: Text and Translation* (1925) are strongly penitential in form conveying an overwhelming sense of a sinful people's utter dependence on God's mercy to deliver them from punishment. The church, as much as the world, was seen as a community of sinners.

Penitence was not, of course, the monopoly of Celtic Christians. It was a very important theme throughout the early mediaeval church in the context of an ever-present emphasis on divine judgement and an overwhelming fear of Hell and damnation. There was a preoccupation with how Christians might be able to atone and receive forgiveness for the sins which they had committed after their baptisms and which risked their salvation and passage to Heaven after the Last Judgement. By the fifth century the church had constructed a complex system of public penances, or set punishments, which enabled errant Christians to obtain remission of their sins and failings.

The early Mediaeval Irish church developed a unique approach to both penitence and penance which was to be highly influential in pastoral care across the western Christian world. It was expressed through monastic Penitentials and rules and through the figure of the *anamchara*, or soul friend. As always, we need to be careful about generalising from the largely monastic sources which we have for the so-called golden age of Celtic Christianity. Penitential attitudes and practices are particularly associated with the monastic vocation. Those who live under vows and rules are especially directed to lives of penitence. Fans of *The Sound of Music* (and who isn't?) will recall that in the song 'How do you solve a problem like Maria' the fact that, in one nun's view at least, 'her penitence is real' more than makes up for the errant postulant's lateness for chapel and meals. For Irish monks, green martyrdom, the most widely practised of the three forms of witness which they sought to follow, involved a life of purgation and penitence based on obedience, abstinence, fasting and prayer. It envisaged the core of the monk's relationship with Christ in terms of penitential activity and renunciation of sin. But it was not just the monks who saw themselves as penitents – so did many of the lay people who flocked to the monasteries in search of healing, forgiveness and resolution of their burdens of guilt and sin. Adomnán described many people with troubled consciences coming to Iona to seek out Columba who established a special penitents' colony on the island of Tiree, to which people were sent often for several years to work out penances appropriate to the sins which they had committed. Jonas of Bobbio similarly recorded crowds flocking to Columbanus to receive the healing power of the *medicamenta penitentiae*. Penitents lived alongside monks in the monasteries working through the penalties prescribed in the Penitentials.

The punishments dished out to penitents often involved exile from their homelands. An Irishman named Lugaid who came to Iona after committing incest with his mother and murdering his brother was sentenced by Columba to lifelong exile from Ireland 'repenting with tears of remorse', beginning with twelve years of penance in a monastery 'among the British'. This was too much for him and after a few days on Iona, he returned to his native land where, as Columba had prophesied, he was killed. Some stories suggest that Columba himself left his own native Ireland as a penitent, exiled because of some crime or misdemeanour which he had committed.

The Penitentials, long lists of sins and lapses of behaviour with the appropriate penalties or punishments needed for their forgiveness, are the largest single category of document surviving from the early centuries of indigenous Christianity in the British Isles. The earliest may actually have been drawn up in Wales but they developed in their most characteristic and influential form in Ireland. Their basis lay in a monastic theology of asceticism. They can seem coldly formulaic and pettily legalistic to our eyes, but they were rooted in a number of insights about both the nature of God and the human condition which are still very relevant today. The fact that for every sin there was an appropriate remedy carried the important message that there is nothing that is beyond redemption or expiation and that there are no limits to divine mercy and forgiveness. The emphasis was on healing the soul through a process of true repentance, confession and forgiveness as much as on punishing the sinner. Penance was seen as the medicine of the soul, every bit as important as the medicine dispensed by physicians to heal the body. The Penitentials, which tackled the eight deadly sins of gluttony, fornication, greed or avarice, pride, despair or despondency, wrath, vainglory and sloth, applied the principle first found among the desert monks of Egypt and Syria and brought to the west through the writings of Cassian, a fifth-century ascetic who founded a monastery in Gaul, of curing by contraries – so those guilty of gluttony were put on diets and those given to over much chatting and gossip endured periods of silence.

The Penitentials imposed radically different punishments on clergy and laity committing the same offence. In the case of the homicide of a neighbour, for example, the Penitential of Finnian laid down that a cleric should live for half a year on a diet of just bread and water and for a further year abstaining from wine and meat. The penance for a layman committing the same offence was a fast of only seven days 'for since he is a man of this world, his guilt is lighter in this world, and his reward less in the world to come'. Simply being on familiar terms with a woman, 'without cohabitation or lascivious embraces', carried the penalty for a cleric of refraining from communion and subsisting on bread and water for forty days.

Penitence, seen as the overcoming of the natural human tendency towards weakness, selfishness and sin, was regarded as a continual process. Penitents moved through a sequence which led from sin, through sorrow and penance, to health, with the emphasis on healing and on the mercy of God, the one ever ready to forgive. This process, conceived almost as a pilgrimage, was not to be undergone in the public gaze, as in the church's system of penances which it challenged and ultimately replaced, but rather in private. At its heart was regular confession as an outward expression of genuine contrition. According to his life, Molua, a sixth-century Irish saint said to have founded several monasteries including Clonfert, taught that 'as the floor is swept every day, so is the soul cleansed every day by confession' (O'Laoghaire 1990: 34). Penitence was a matter of persistence, a constant wiping of the slate clean by God. An early Irish poem, possibly dating from the seventh century and attributed to Mancháin Léith, commended this gradualist approach: 'The path of repentance, if anyone should take, let him advance a step a day and not practise the ways of a charioteer' (O'Laoghaire 1990: 35). Penitence was thus seen as both a gradual and also a cyclical process, involving constant departing and constant resolve to return. There was a recognition of the human tendency to backslide and stumble. In the words of Thomas O'Loughlin:

> The challenge that the Christianity of the early medieval Celtic peoples offers us – and this is something that is distinctive to them – is a view of sin and healing, and the idea that Christian living is a journey where we have to take up our pack each day and set out in discipleship. Christianity has always preached conversion/penitence/metanoia as its

basic call, but equally it has always had difficulties with the idea of clearing the slate and starting again. This is a human need. The insular practice of penitence was not perhaps the best possible, but it was a massive improvement on what went before it. It recognised that one did not become a disciple in one or two dramatic moves, but in a whole series, where 'downs' followed 'ups': the whole process should be seen as ongoing therapy rather than as a punitive repayment of debts.
(O'Loughlin Journeys 2000: 154-5)

Although in the understanding expressed in the Irish Penitentials, penance was a private and internal matter, essentially between the conscience of the individual and God, the penitent was not alone. His or her soul friend stood alongside, combining the roles of mentor, confessor, spiritual guide, buddy and companion in adversity. It was to some extent a mutual relationship. In this context, the Penitentials were handbooks for confessors or physicians of the soul who used them to steer people away from harmful and destructive behaviour.

The figure of the soul friend, or *anamchara* to use the Irish term, is one of the most distinctive in Celtic Christianity and also one of the most lauded today. Like so many other aspects of Irish monasticism, it derived from the desert monasticism of Egypt and Syria in the third and fourth centuries, and specifically from the practice of each monk having a cell mate, either in the literal sense of someone sharing his cramped living and sleeping space or in the more figurative sense of a special buddy and companion. Every Irish monk seems to have had his own soul friend whom he had chosen of his own volition. The monastic rules laid down criteria as to both the qualities required and the duties of soul friends. The eighth-century Rule of Tallaght prescribed that they should be 'learned in the rule of conduct laid down in Scripture and in the rules of the saints' and that their role was 'to correct all impiety, without harshness, without shame; correction of all the proud with humility and with laughter'. Soul friends were enjoined 'You do well to correct. You do not do well to reprove. The mind rebels against reproof. It is humble at being corrected'. On the whole, soul friends seem to have been older than those to whom they acted as advisers, mentors and spiritual directors. They did not need to be ordained priests. Three female nuns, Brigid, Ide and

Samhthann, were particularly noted for their guidance of souls. Brigid is credited with the much-quoted observation that 'a person without a soul friend is like a body without a head'.

It is clear that the system of soul friends was widespread if not universal within Celtic monasteries and nunneries. What is much less clear is how far it was taken up in the world beyond the monastic *vallum*. It is worth noting that Brigid's remark was made to a young ordained monk. Kings and princes seem to have had soul friends who acted as counsellors and advisers, but it seems unlikely that the more humble Christians living in the scattered townships of the British Isles in the early mediaeval period would have had individual spiritual companions and guides on the monastic model. That may well have been why they had recourse to well-known and respected spiritual directors like Columba and Columbanus when they felt burdened with sin or guilt. Special provision does seem to have been made for the young. The Life of Colman noted that children who had been baptized and confirmed were taken to soul friends with whom they read the Psalms. The practice of fostering out the sons and daughters of high-born Irish families to monks and nuns known for their skills of discernment and mentoring is well attested and seems to have led to many of these young charges taking up the dedicated religious life themselves. Certain individuals seem to have been identified almost as generic soul friends, in the sense of being recognised mentors and counsellors to whom lay people would go when in spiritual need and trouble. An eighth century rule advised that 'to go to a devout sage is good, to direct one's path. A devout sage to guide you, it is good to avoid punishment'.

Once again, we are frustrated by the fact that so few of our sources for this period come from outside the monastic context. It would be fascinating to know how far the principles and practice of soul friendship extended across Celtic Christian communities as a whole. Even if they were largely confined to monasteries, the existence of the *anamchairde* and the importance attached to them, point to significant features of the Irish approach to penitence. It was not to be undertaken alone but rather in the company of another in a relationship which was to some extent mutual even if there was an understanding that the soul friend possessed special wisdom and powers of guidance and discernment. Reflecting on its origins in desert monasticism, and on the fact that 'every Christian must, in some sense, experience a wandering in the desert', Hugh Connolly has this to say about the distinctive Celtic approach to penitence as revealed in the Irish Penitentials and the figure of the *anamchara*:

> The penitentials are really the handbooks of the desert experience. In this model, the minister is viewed above all as the fellow-traveller, fellow-pilgrim, fellow-sufferer, or, to use the Celtic term, *anamchara* (soul-friend). The emphasis in this model is predominantly on solidarity. Both minister and penitent are, ultimately, both pilgrims on the same pilgrim path. The important thing is to persevere, to remain steadfast, to stand ready and even to do battle with the forces of evil. Thus, a secondary image becomes that of battle. The Celtic values of heroism and valour are put to work in the struggle against sin and vice.
>
> But man is also morally weak, fragile, incomplete. He needs support and sustenance. Hence, the role of the *anamchara* who receives the weary pilgrim with hospitality and restores him. Here the emphasis is placed, not so much on the saving judgement or salutary medicine but on the fraternal witness and compassion of the *anamchara*. The notion of Celtic or green martyrdom is uppermost here; one must bear *living* witness to the Gospel. And the trait *par excellence* of this testimony is spiritual humility, *paupertas* (Patrick) or *humilitas* (Columbanus).
>
> (Connolly 1995:178)

Although we may find it difficult to grasp, the Irish penitential system was seen as positive, life-giving, curative and healing rather than as the embodiment of a negative fixation on sin and judgement and a preoccupation with punishment. It reflected an emphasis in Celtic Christianity on God's love as much as on divine judgement. It is summed up in the 'four redemptions of the soul' described in the *Alphabet of Devotion* attributed to the late sixth century Irish monk Colmán mac Béognae: 'fear and repentance, love and hope'. The positive aspect of penance, seen in terms of healing rather than as a dry and harsh system of punishments, is well expressed in the thirteenth century Welsh poem, *The Loves of Taliesin*, which returns again and again to 'the beauty of doing penance for sin and excess' in the context of a long catalogue of other beautiful things, such as mead, beer, leeks and elegant Welsh.

Unlike some of the later mediaeval developments based around formal confession to a priest, penances and indulgences, the theology underlying the Irish Penitentials was emphatically not a matter of fulfilling formulaic requirements or earning merit through doing works. To quote Hugh Connolly again, 'it was not as though one somehow earned forgiveness through penitential activity; rather, in the practice of therapeutic sacrifice, one re-discovered in one's heart God's call to forgiveness'. (Connolly,1995, p.15).

As Connolly suggests, for all its apparent harshness to modern eyes, the Irish penitential system displayed pastoral sensitivity, acknowledging human weakness and the constant tendency to backslide and relapse. In contrast to the prevailing view in the early mediaeval western church, it conceived of penance as a repeatable action, not a one-off unrepeatable event. Reconciliation with God was viewed as a life-long process of therapy and healing. While it was important to work out the appropriate proscribed penalty, punishment and satisfaction required for an offence, understood as a price to be paid or the settlement of a debt and described as *poena*, it was equally if not more important to overcome sin, or *culpa*, by the inner conviction of a truly contrite heart full of sorrow and genuine repentance. There are many references in early Celtic sources to the penance of tears. Rhygfarch describes David as 'overflowing with daily fountains of tears'; a ninth century Irish prayer begins 'God, give me a well of tears, my sins to hide, or I am left like arid earth unsanctified'; and a tenth century prayer asks:

> Grant me tears, O Lord, to blot out my sins;
> May I not cease from them, O God, until I have been purified.
> Grant me tears in bed to moisten my pillow,
> So that his dear ones may help cure the soul.

It is not too much to say that the principles introduced and expressed in the Irish Penitentials changed the whole western approach to moral theology and specifically to the practice of penance. They initiated a new way of looking at sin, forgiveness and reconciliation and a system of private rather than public confession. Sin was henceforth seen primarily as a disease, with penance being seen as a medicine rather than a punishment.

Although the Irish system of private penance was taken over in the mediaeval Catholic church, vital elements such as the emphasis on genuine contrition of the heart as expressed through tears, the role of the soul friend and the on-going gradual nature of penitence were lost. Penance became a somewhat mechanical sacrament focused on penitent and priest in the Confessional. The development of the idea of Purgatory and the practice of offering indulgences brought a renewed emphasis on *poena* and its commutation or mitigation at the expense of true repentance, as expressed in Jesus' words in Mark 1.15 'The Kingdom of God is at hand. Repent and believe the good news'. Although the Reformation corrected some of these deviations, it did not quite bring a return to the distinctive Celtic focus on penitence, with its emphasis on the importance of inner contrition as much as outer penance, on the constant continuum leading not just once but again and again from sin, through sorrow and penance, to health, and on the mercy of God, the one ever ready to forgive.

2 PRAISE

The theme of praise of the Trinitarian God echoes through the prayers, poems, liturgies and saints' lives which form our main sources for accessing and understanding Celtic Christianity. This is hardly surprising given the monastic origins of virtually all these texts. Continual praise of God and his wondrous acts is the central work of a monastic community, constantly enjoined and reinforced for the Irish monks by the Psalms which were at the heart of their daily and nightly worship. Among the most pronounced characteristics of the Island of Delights in the *Brendan Voyage* was the fact that, although scattered around the island, 'the monks lived with one mind and heart in faith, hope and love, sharing a common table and remaining always united in singing the praise of God'.

But it was more than just the monastic context that made praise so central to Christians in the Celtic-speaking regions of the British Isles in the early Middle Ages. It is clear that for them being a Christian was not primarily a matter of following a philosophy, subscribing to a set of doctrines or participating in a cult with certain rituals but rather of joining other people and indeed the whole of creation in acknowledging dependence on God, being held in divine love and expressing spontaneous praise and thanksgiving for this state. Voicing praise, through prayer and song, was regarded alongside constant repentance and acts of mercy and charity as one of the authentic signs of Christian life.

Praise was seen very much as a corporate rather than an individual attitude and act. Again, the monastic influence was clearly important here but so too was the sense of the closeness of the cloud of witnesses and hosts of heaven and the theme of pleroma explored in the last chapter. Praise linked the worshipping community on earth with the hosts of heaven, envisaged in being engaged in continual praise of God, and indeed the whole created order. Indeed, the praise being continually offered up in heaven and by the animals and birds on earth called and encouraged humans to a similar attitude. An early Irish poem begins:

> Only a fool would fail
> To praise God in his might,
> When the tiny mindless birds
> Praise Him in their flight

It is within the Welsh tradition that this attitude of praise is most clearly and constantly expressed. I have already alluded to the ninth century Welsh poem which contains the line 'It is not too great a toil to praise the Trinity' and ends 'It is not too great a toil to praise the Son of Mary'. A Welsh poem dating from the tenth or eleventh century in the *Black Book of Carmarthen* begins:

> In the name of the Lord, mine to praise, of great praise,
> I shall praise God, great the triumph of his love.

Other poems in this collection enjoin praise of God at the beginning and end of every day and describe all the elements of the natural world, including plain and hillside, springs, cedars, fruit trees, birds, bees and the grass of the field continually praising God. This tradition of praise poetry has continued right up to the present in the Welsh language.

Closely allied to this emphasis on praise was an affirmation of the importance of blessing and benediction. The lives of the Celtic saints are full of instances where they bless people, animals or even inanimate objects, sometimes by making the sign of the cross but often by speaking words of blessing. Adomnán describes Columba blessing a fruit tree, a block of salt, a pail of milk and a small round stone from a river as well as his monks and the island of Iona and its inhabitants. There appears to have been an emphasis on benediction in early Celtic liturgies. The *Antiphonary of Bangor* accords a central place to the Benedicite, the ancient Jewish hymn which calls on the elements of creation to bless the Lord. According to some authorities, Irish eucharists seem to have been characterized by the frequency of episcopal blessings during the course of the service. People are described as coming to Irish and Welsh monasteries not just for counselling and to be prescribed the medicine of penance but also simply to be blessed. In part, this is a reflection of the power of the spoken word throughout Celtic society. Until the coming of Christianity, Celtic culture was entirely oral, not just because of widespread illiteracy but also because the act of writing down a word or phrase was regarded as destroying its potency and effectiveness. Something of this attitude persisted into Celtic Christian culture even though Christianity was the religion of the Word and the book and the monks were busy in their scriptoria writing down traditional poems and sayings as well as copying the Gospels and the Psalms.

Celtic saints were renowned for cursing as well as blessing. In both cases, they were conforming to this cultural tradition of the force and power of the spoken word. Blessing was much more common than cursing. It tied in with the disposition towards praise. As Donald Allchin has observed in considering the close relationship between the roles of priest and poet in the Welsh tradition, 'to bless (*benedicere*) in its original meaning is to speak good things, to declare the goodness which is latent in the world around us, when that world is seen and known as the world of God.' (Allchin 1991:6). I devoted a whole chapter to blessing and cursing in my book *Colonies of Heaven: Celtic Models for Today's Church* (Bradley 2000: 58-87) and I refer the reader there for a fuller discussion of this interesting topic. Here, let me simply note the closeness of blessing and praise and echo the sentiments of Saunders Lewis, the great twentieth century Welsh Christian poet who summed up both the specifically Welsh tradition of praise poetry and the wider Celtic emphasis on both these themes in the simple affirmation at the end of one of his poems 'Praise to his name, all praise' (quoted Allchin 1997: 140).

3 POVERTY

Christ's call to poverty, understood in both material and spiritual terms, seems to have been heeded especially seriously by both British and Irish Christians in the early Middle Ages. Patrick described his own state as that of *paupertas* and wrote in his *Confessio* 'Poverty and woe are more my line than pleasures and riches – after all, Christ the Lord was poor for our sake'. The early Irish hymn, 'Be Thou my vision' expresses a similar theme in its line 'Riches I heed not nor man's empty praise'. Clearly resonating here were Jesus' call on those who would be his disciples to give away their money and not stack up material possessions for themselves, his own self-description of the Son of Man having nowhere to lay his head, and his blessing of the poor in spirit in the Sermon on the Mount.

Poverty was a favourite theme in the sermons and theological writings that have come down to us from the golden age of Celtic Christianity. A fifth-century tract 'On Riches' attributed to Pelagius was clear in its message:

> In what manner are we to imitate Christ? In poverty, if I am not mistaken, not in riches; in humility, not in pride; not in worldly glory; by despising money, not coveting it. And what are the commandments of the new covenant that we are to keep? First and foremost, those by which the occasion of sin is to be removed through contempt of riches. That is why you will find that the Lord gave no commandment to those who desire to follow him and to offer themselves as his disciples which was of higher priority than to despise riches and the world.
>
> (Rees 1991:187).

In his *De Excidio Britanniae* Gildas wrote:

> The Lord calls the poor blessed, not the haughty poor, not those who despise the brethren, but the meek. Not the envious but those who weep for their own or others' sins; not those who hunger and thirst for water with scorn of other men, but those who hunger and thirst for righteousness; not those who condemn others, but the merciful; not the proud, but the peacemakers.
>
> (Connolly 1995: 24-25)

A similar message is found in Columbanus' sermons:

> Let us share with the poor, that even so we may deserve to
> share with the poor in that place where they shall be satisfied
> who here for Christ's sake hunger and thirst for righteousness.
> For to whom belongs the kingdom of heaven save to the poor?
>
> (Walker :93)

The Irish monastic rules emphasized poverty more than either
chastity or obedience. Comgall's Rule put it simply: 'love Christ,
hate wealth'. Monks following the Rule of Columcille were
commanded 'be always naked in imitation of Christ'. This was
later spelled out in terms of an attitude of renunciation and
abstinence in respect of possessions, clothing, food, drink and
property. The Rule of Columbanus had a section 'On Poverty
and Overcoming Greed':

> Monks, to whom for Christ's sake the world is crucified as they
> are to the world, must avoid greed when it is not only wrong
> for them to have things superfluous to their needs but also to
> desire them. In that case it is not possessions that are required
> but will; taking a leave of all things and every day following
> the Lord Christ with a cross of fear, they have treasure in
> heaven. Therefore, while they shall have much in heaven,
> they should be satisfied on earth with the bare minimum,
> knowing that greed is a leprosy for monks who imitate the
> sons of the prophets, for the disciple of Christ it is betrayal
> and ruin, and for the uncertain followers of the Apostles also
> it is death. Thus nakedness and disdain of riches are the first
> perfection of the monk.
>
> (Davies 1999: 248).

Stories of the Celtic monks suggest that they followed out these
precepts. Rhigyfach wrote that the monks in David's monastery
'loved poverty of their own free will' and that anyone entering the
monastic life renounced everything 'and was received naked, as
if escaping from a shipwreck'. Aidan gave away the gifts that he
received from King Oswyn and others to poor people whom he
met as he walked around his Northumbrian diocese. The king,
concerned that Aidan was walking everywhere, gave him a fine
horse. Soon afterwards, Aidan met a beggar who asked him for

alms. The saint dismounted and handed the horse over to the poor man. The theme of kenosis, or self-emptying, looms large in the lives of the Celtic saints. It is perhaps significant that many of them came from wealthy aristocratic backgrounds. Their decision to become monks, and the kind of lives they cultivated, represented a deliberate renunciation of the wealth and power which they would naturally have had given their status and breeding. Their stories are very similar to that of St Francis of Assisi, the son of a wealthy merchant who gave up all his wealth and married 'Lady Poverty' to follow Christ.

This attitude of material poverty went alongside the cultivation of a spiritual poverty in direct imitation of Jesus' words in the Beatitudes 'Blessed are the poor in spirit'. This was understood as a call to live a life of utter humility and service. The old Irish Life of Columba portrays the saint taking off the sandals of his tired monks in order to wash their feet, bringing their share of corn in from the fields on his own back and grinding it for them. Humility was taken very seriously and almost literally in terms of its original meaning of being close to the ground or earth (*humus* and *humilis* in Latin). The Welsh word *iselder* means lowliness – it also means depression. The monks' sense of humility was part of that rigorous austerity captured in the Rule of Colmcille:

> Follow almsgiving before all things,
> Take not of food till thou are hungry,
> Sleep not till thou feelest desire,
> Speak not except on business.

Pride was the great sin to be avoided at all costs. Christians should be humble, lowly and not puffed up in any way, nor scorning small acts of service and kindness. In his last sermon David reputedly told his monks to 'do the little things, the small things you've seen me doing'. Such an outlook was not, of course, peculiar to Celtic Christianity. We can find it well expressed in the writings of several of the great Christian mystics. Teresa of Avila famously observed that 'God lives also among the pots and pans' and Thérèse of Lisieux wrote that 'the Lord needs from us neither great deeds nor profound thoughts. Neither intelligence nor talents. He cherishes simplicity.' Celtic Christianity stood very clearly in this tradition of affirming spiritual as well as material poverty and affirming the value of 'the little things' as much as the big spectacular actions.

4 PROPHECY

In the introduction to his life of Columba Adomnán outlined its division into three parts: 'The first will contain Prophetic Revelations; the second Divine Miracles performed by him; the third will contain Angelic Apparitions and certain manifestations of heavenly brightness upon the man of God.' It is significant that in this particular trinity, prophecy came before manifestations of divine power and heavenly presences. If their biographers are to be believed, prophecy was a major activity of the Celtic saints, understood both in terms of foretelling future events in line with the gifts of the Spirit as outlined by St Paul and also in terms of speaking truth to power in the manner of the Old Testament prophets.

Prophesying seems to have been far more important to the Celtic saints than preaching. With the notable exception of Columbanus, none of them have left sermons and they were seldom portrayed as preaching either in the monasteries or outside them. By contrast they were frequently described as exercising gifts of the spirit such as prophecy, healing and performing other miraculous signs and wonders. Columba was the supreme exemplar in this regard. In the introduction to the first part of his life Adomnán wrote:

> He began as a young man to enjoy the spirit of prophecy, to predict the future and to tell those with him about things happening elsewhere. He could see what was done afar off, because he was there in the spirit though not in the body. One time when a few of the brethren pressed him about this, the man of the Lord, St Columba, did not deny that by divine grace he had several times experienced a miraculous enlarging of the grasp of the mind so that he seemed to look at the whole world caught in one ray of sunlight.
>
> (Sharpe 1995:112)

As recounted by Adomnán, Columba's prophecies included foretelling how people were going to develop and change in character and predicting the outcomes of battles, impending deaths, weather patterns, including the sudden onset of storms, and natural disasters as far away as Italy. He was several times portrayed as correctly identifying who would succeed to a disputed throne or who would appear as an unexpected guest on Iona, like the crane whom he foresaw flying over from the north of Ireland. Some of his prophecies seem rather trivial, as when he predicted that a book would fall into a pail of water or that a clumsy visitor would knock over his ink horn and spill the ink in it.

It is hard to know what to make of this long litany of prophecies and predictions – fifty in all are mentioned and described by Adomnán as 'only a few out of many'. It is not surprising that on the basis of them Columba has been hailed as a Druid-like seer blessed with psychic and paranormal powers, perhaps indeed the first person to be credited with the second sight that is associated with the Gaelic temperament. But there may be a much more overtly Christian explanation for these apparently pagan powers. James Bruce argues that Columba's prophecies, like his miracles, are related to Adomnán's eschatological emphasis on the coming of the kingdom. He sees them very much as gifts of the Spirit and proofs of the flowering of faith which manifest the coming of the kingdom of God: 'For Adomnán, it is the Holy Spirit, the Spirit of prophecy, who empowers and enables this prophetic activity, and the accounts of prophecy play a dominant part in Adomnán's presentation of the role of the Spirit in the life and ministry of Columba.' (Bruce 2004:202). Although none of Columba's prophecies refer to the last days, judgement or the end times, Bruce is quite sure that they carry an eschatological meaning and significance:

> We do see in them the inexorable progress of the establishment of the rule of God amongst those who come into contact with this harbinger of the kingdom, and we see that in the very act of prophesying by the Holy Spirit, Columba is realizing the biblically prophesied conditions of the kingdom themselves foretold by the prophet Joel and claimed by the apostle Peter.
> (Bruce 2004: 203)

What is particularly interesting is Adomnán's remark in the introduction to the first part of the Life of Columba about the saint on occasions being present in the spirit though not in the body. Several examples of this are given in the *Vita*. A fascinating story, which has been compared to the risen Jesus' encounter with two of his disciples on the road to Emmaus, tells of a group of monks returning to the monastery on Iona after a day working on the harvest in the fields on the western side of the island. When they were half way home, despite being exhausted by their labours they suddenly felt a sense of elation and well-being. They begged Columba's cousin Baithéne to explain to them what was the cause of this wonderful relief. He explained:

> You know that our elder, Columba, thinks anxiously about us, and is upset when we return home to him so late, for he knows we are hard at work. And so it is that, since he may not come to meet us in the body, his spirit meets us as we walk and refreshes us in this way so that we are joyful.
>
> (Sharpe 1995: 140).

Such out of the body experiences were by no means uncommon in the lives of the Celtic saints. There is a particularly dramatic example in the life of Fursey (c.597-649), the first recorded Irish missionary to Anglo-Saxon England and associated with the evangelization of East Anglia. The first published work about him, *Transitus Beati Fursei*, which dates from either the late seventh or early eighth century, described a series of visions which amounted to what would nowadays be described as either out of the body or near death experiences. They included a heavenly vision where he saw angels and heard extraordinary music coming from the beating of their wings and their singing, a vision of a cosmic battle between the hosts of heaven and a cloud of foul black devils described in somewhat similar terms to the appearance of the Dementors in the *Harry Potter* films, and a frightening glimpse of the eternal fires of Hell. While the hosts of heaven eventually triumphed in the battle which Fursey witnessed, the overwhelming sense with which he was left when he came back into his body was that the end of the world was nigh.

It is hard to overstate this apocalyptic eschatological element in the thinking of Celtic Christians as revealed in their prayers and other writings. We have already noted it in the *Altus Prosator* with its powerful evocation of the imminence of the second coming of Christ to judge the world. Columba, like Fursey, had visions of a cosmic battle being waged between angels and foul black devils in the sky over his head. Across the church in the early Christian centuries there was a widespread feeling of living in the last days and the imminent end of the world. Such sentiments are certainly clearly evident in the sources that have come down to us from the golden age of the Celtic saints.

Alongside their exercise of prophecy as a gift of the Spirit and harbinger of the last days, the Celtic saints were also portrayed as exercising a very different kind of prophetic ministry much more akin to that practised by the Old Testament prophets of calling rulers to account and speaking truth to power. This was highlighted in the relationship between Aidan and his close friends and patrons Oswald and Oswyn, successive kings of Northumbria. It is clear from what Bede wrote of them that Aidan served as a kind of counsellor and instructor to both, telling them to look after the poor and act with mercy and justice. When Aidan gave away to a beggar the fine horse that Oswyn had specially chosen for him, the king was understandably miffed, as Bede recounted:

> Happening to meet the bishop as they were going to dinner, he said, 'my lord bishop, why did you want to give a beggar the royal horse intended for you? Have we not many less valuable horses or other things which would have been good enough to give to the poor, without letting the beggar have the horse which I had specially chosen for your own use?' The bishop at once replied, 'O King, what are you saying? Surely this son of a mare is not dearer to you than the son of God?' After these words they went in to dine. The bishop sat down in his own place and the king, who had just come in from hunting, stood warming himself by the fire with his thegns. Suddenly he remembered the bishop's words; and at once he took off his sword, gave it to a thegn, and then hastening to where the bishop sat, threw himself at his feet and asked his pardon. 'Never from henceforth', he said, 'will I speak of this again nor will I form any opinion as to what money of mine or how much of it you should give to the sons of God.'
>
> (Bede 1999:133)

There is a wonderful mixture of both kinds of prophecy in a story that Bede told of Oswald sitting down to dinner with Aidan and a silver dish being placed on the table before him full of rich foods. On being told by a servant that a great multitude of the poor among his subjects were outside asking for alms, the king immediately ordered the dainties which had been set in front of him to be carried to the poor and the silver dish to be broken up into pieces and divided among them. Aidan, delighted with this pious act, grasped Oswald by the right hand and said, 'May this hand never decay'. Bede continued: 'His blessing and his prayer were fulfilled in this way: when Oswald was killed in battle, his hand and arm were cut off from the rest of his body, and they have remained uncorrupt until this present time; they are in fact preserved in a silver shrine in St Peter's church in the royal city which is called Bamburgh.' (Bede 1999:119).

In that story both kinds of prophecy – foretelling the future and admonishing the powerful – come together and serve as a reminder of the importance of following the injunction in Micah 6.8 that what God requires of us is to act justly, love mercy and walk humbly with him.

5 PATIENCE/PERSEVERANCE

The linked virtues of patience and perseverance were much lauded in the writings of early Celtic Christians. Patience was seen as an essential attribute of faith and went with a sense of acceptance and resignation. In his *Confessio* Patrick reflected, 'So whatever happens to me – good or ill – I ought to accept with an even temper and always give thanks to God who has shown me that I can trust him without limit or doubt'. The story of Brendan's voyage could be taken as an allegory extolling the virtues of perseverance. Before setting out Brendan and his 14 companions completed a 40 day fast in three day periods. Their journey across the ocean visiting the many islands along the way took over seven years. When they finally reached the promised land of the saints they were told, 'this is the land which you have sought for so long. You were not able to find it immediately because God wished to show you his many wonders in the great ocean'.

The value of waiting and the importance of cultivating an attitude of patience were strongly inculcated among monks. Anyone seeking to enter David's monastery in south west Wales had first to remain for ten days outside the doors. Rhigyfach noted, 'If he exercised patience and stood there until the tenth day, he was first admitted and put to serve under the elder who had charge of the gate. When he had laboured there for a good while, and resistance in his soul had been broken down, he was finally judged to be ready to enter the company of the brethren' (Davies 1999:200). Monastic rules emphasized the importance of perseverance. Ailbe's rule symbolized the strength and personal discipline required for it as 'a striking of the anvil into the block, to be there until death' (Thom 200:93). The Rule of Comgall laid down that 'in every desire which thou desirest thou shouldst exercise patience' (Thom 200:98).

There was a matching conviction that patience was also a significant attribute of God. Pelagius expressed this clearly in his letter 'On the Christian life' addressed to a Christian widow. It contained a long reflection on divine patience which pointed out that God does not punish sinners immediately nor judge rashly but in his great patience gives them time to repent. Pelagius commended God's long suffering in making the erring human race the object of his continuing concern, 'for were he not patient, the stock of the human race would have come to an end long ago, nor would we find sinners turning into righteous men if God were willing to punish sinners out of hand'. In common with other Celtic Christians, Pelagius was in no doubt about the terrible reality of divine judgement but he also felt that:

> God does not remit the penalty for sin but only delays its punishment nor does he free the persistent sinner from death but waits patiently, so that he may be converted, though late, and live....Good, kind and merciful as he is, he does not strike you at once, wanting you to recognize how great is his mercy and goodness towards you and preferring to wait the repentance of the sinner and the ungodly and thus save a sinner when converted rather than punish him while still in sin.

> (Rees 1991: 108-9)

This is an interesting statement. While acknowledging the importance of divine judgement and human penitence and repentance, themes that would one expect to be highlighted by one schooled in the principles of Celtic monasticism, it also emphasizes God's infinite patience which is in a real sense what preserves us and saves us. God does not condemn people while they are still in sin but rather waits until they have reflected and repented. It is an important corrective to the rather hard view of God that we find in much early Celtic writing. Here it is God's patience, allied to his goodness, kindness and mercy, which is being emphasized. How representative Pelagius was in espousing this view it is difficult to establish but we can link it to the emphasis on patience and perseverance in Irish monastic writings and not least in the Irish Penitentials where, as we have seen, coming to terms with and overcoming the human tendency to sin was viewed as a continual, on-going almost lifelong process, conceived in terms of healing rather than punishment.

6 PRACTICAL ACTION

As has already been noted, the writings left by Celtic-speaking Christians in the British Isles in the early Middle Ages suggest that they had little time for endless speculation about God and what would nowadays be called systematic or philosophical theology. Their focus lay rather on prayer and praise and also on practical action.

The lives of the Celtic saints portray them as devoting themselves to good works. According to Rhigyfach, David 'spent all day, one after another, steadfastly and untiringly teaching, praying and kneeling, and caring for his brethren as well as feeding a host of orphans, wards, widows, the sick, the weak and pilgrims' (Davies 1999:200). Rhigyfach also commented that Patrick 'refurbished the lamp of fruitful endeavour with the oil of double charity'. Irish monastic rules enjoined monks to undertake practical good works, not least hospitality and caring for the poor and sick. The *Alphabet of Devotion* began by extolling 'faith with action' and went on to enumerate among those things which should be learned and practised by Christians 'tending the sick' and 'compassion to a neighbour'.

There was a similar strong emphasis on practical good works in a collection of seven model Hiberno-Latin sermons possibly dating from the early eighth century which were probably used by Irish monks when they went out preaching and teaching in the scattered townships beyond the monasteries. They preached that good works would count as much as faith on the Day of Judgement. The second sermon asked:

> For what were you born into the world? For what other than that you should do good? And if you do something through ignorance or stupid contrariness, it is necessary that you amend for this through a good work. If the last day finds you with these good works, then the angels will greet you and

will receive you with joy, and they will lead you before the tribunal of judgement, there you will receive according as you have done.'

(O'Loughlin Journeys 2000:120-121)

The fourth sermon reflected on Jesus' well-known words in Matthew 6.33, 'Seek ye first the kingdom of God':

> So one should first seek the kingdom through good works, that is charity and fasting and prayer and humility and benevolence; and whatever we need, that will be placed before us, and he gives us immortality and eternal life for good works. God does not seek the start of the work but its end.

(O'Loughlin Journeys 2000:126-7)

This seems to come very near to expressing a doctrine of salvation through good works as much as if not even more than through faith. This is also the strong impression given in the writings of Pelagius who appears to argue that it is not what you believe that matters but rather what you do, in terms of becoming like Christ and following his teaching rather than just believing in and worshipping him. In his letter 'On the Christian life' he strongly made the point that it is no good simply possessing the name and being called a Christian.

> No one is assigned any name whatever without due cause: to be called a cobbler it is necessary to produce shoes; it is his skill in a craft that causes a man to be called an artificer or craftsman; for a man to be called a businessman he sells at a higher price what he has bought more cheaply. For it is by examples of this kind that we recognize that there is no name without an act but that every name comes from an act.
>
> How can you then be called a Christian, if there is no Christian act in you? Christian is the name for righteousness, goodness, integrity, forbearance, chastity, prudence, humility, kindness, blamelessness, godliness. How can you defend and appropriate that name, when not even a few of these many qualities abide in you? He is a Christian who is one not only in name but in deed, who imitates and follows Christ in everything, who is holy, guiltless, undefiled, unstained, in whose breast malice has no place, in whose breast only

116

godliness and goodness reside, who does not know how to hurt or harm anyone but only how to help everyone.

(Rees 1991: 112-3)

Later in the same letter Pelagius attacked those whose 'ignorance of their own folly and imprudence so cheats and deceives that they form the opinion that the faith which they pretend to have will profit them before God without works of righteousness'. This attitude, he suggested, came from a false understanding 'that God is the avenger not of crimes but only of faithlessness'. (Rees 1991: 120). In another letter sometimes attributed to Pelagius but more likely to have been written by one of his disciples, 'On Bad Teachers', the epistle of James was cited to show that it is only through works that we show our faith and that faith on its own cannot save us:

So you see that a man is justified by works and not by faith alone. Profession of faith will be of profit for the Glory of eternal life only to those who can show that they have faith by the practice of good works and by the witness of the holy life, but that it will not be sufficient to win the privilege of such a life for those who have defiled their lives by the shameful pollution of their sins and the disgraceful filth of their misdeeds.

(Rees 1991:221).

This is an unequivocal statement of the doctrine of salvation by works. Whether it is also an assertion of Pelagianism in the sense that the term is usually used – to express the idea that salvation can be achieved through our own individual human efforts and without dependence on God's grace – is much more debatable. I can find no statement in either the writings attributed to Pelagius himself or in other sources from early insular Christianity in the British Isles that salvation can be achieved other than through the grace of God. Divine forgiveness was regarded as crucial to salvation but so also was a demonstration of faith through works, a turning away from sin and a life lived according to the teachings and example of Christ. There is a clear sense in all the sources that I have quoted that faith on its own is not enough, just as it is not enough to call oneself a Christian without following Christ in deed rather than just in name, by loving your neighbour, helping the poor and needy, feeding the hungry, sustaining the widow and the orphan. These practical good works lay at the heart of what was understood as authentic Christianity not just on the part of monks and nuns leading a dedicated, intentional religious life but also in terms of what was preached beyond the monasteries. Practical action was at the very heart of Celtic Christianity.

7
Ways to follow

1 PASTORAL PRESENCE

The theme of presence was important in pastoral terms as well as being key to the way God was envisaged and understood in Celtic Christianity. Those living and working in the monasteries of the British Isles in the early mediaeval period expressed their Christian faith as much through being there alongside people as through evangelizing them. Availability and empathy were regarded as just as valuable as missionary endeavours, if not more so.

This pastoral approach is well illustrated in the life and ministry of Columba. Bede's description of him as a missionary 'preaching the word of God to the province of the northern Picts' has led to a very distorted popular view of him as the almost single-handed evangelist of Scotland who dashed around the country converting the heathen Picts to Christianity. Adomnán, who was much closer to Columba both temporally and geographically than Bede, did not portray him as a missionary but rather as a monk and a pastor, largely based on Iona where he devoted himself first and foremost to prayer and study and then to guiding his monks, healing the sick, aiding the poor and receiving, blessing and counselling visitors who came to the island as pilgrims and penitents. This emphasis on pastoral care seems to have characterized Celtic monks in general. They practised a ministry of presence, witnessing to the Lord not just by rushing around proselytizing and preaching but simply by being there, available when needed.

There was nothing unique about this ministry of pastoral presence exercised by the Irish, Scottish, Welsh and British monasteries. As Benedicta Ward has observed, 'monastic life supplied pastoral care in all its forms to Christian Europe for over 1000 years' (Evans 2000:77). The Anglo-Saxon minster fulfilled a similar role and was the main provider of pastoral care in England before the development of parishes. But the Celtic monasteries do seem to have had a particular investment and interest in this kind of ministry. Even someone as sceptical about the distinctiveness of a 'Celtic Christianity' as Wendy Davies acknowledges in her article 'the Myth of the Celtic Church' that the pastoral outreach to the local community in terms of baptism, burial and spiritual counselling was almost certainly stronger in the Christian communities of Ireland, Scotland and Wales than in continental monasteries. Indeed, she is prepared to concede that this may even count as a distinct characteristic of Celtic Christianity as a whole. (Davies 1992:15)

This pastoral outreach was expressed in a ministry of hospitality. Irish monks washed the feet of visitors in imitation of Jesus' action with his disciples at the last supper. The *hospitium*, or guest house, stood in a prime position in every monastic compound and provided more comfortable accommodation and much better food than the monks themselves had in their own simpler dormitories and refectory. The exercise of this ministry involved a good deal of listening and quiet and patient healing of broken souls. The approach taken by the monks was to get alongside and seek to help people rather than to judge them. As we have seen, judgement was a major theme in early monastic prayers and poems and there is no escaping its centrality as an attribute of God in the Celtic Christian mind. Yet when it came to the exercise of pastoral care, the lives of the saints and accounts of the monks' activities show a non-judgmental approach in which skills of discernment and what would nowadays be called non-directive counselling were to the fore. This approach is illustrated in Adomnán's story of the wife who came to Columba because she could no longer face sleeping with her ugly husband. She hoped that he would tell her to cross the sea and join a women's monastery but in fact he got her and her husband to fast with him for a day. While they slept the following evening he prayed over them and the next day the woman awoke transformed and announced, 'the husband whom I hated I love today. My heart was changed from loathing to love.' (Sharpe 1995:195). Another example is provided by Bede's description of Aidan upbraiding the first Irish cleric sent in response to Oswald's request for a bishop of Lindisfarne for being too harsh in his preaching and approach to the Northumbrians: 'You did not first offer them the milk of simple teaching'. Aidan replaced this first unsuccessful nominee as bishop and proved himself, in Bede's words, to be 'pre-eminently endowed with the grace of discretion which is the mother of all virtues'. Bede also singled out Aidan's qualities of gentleness, moderation and good sense.

The pastoral approach taken by the Celtic saints involved a combination of what would nowadays be called skills of reconciliation, discernment, counselling and spiritual accompaniment. This last form of ministry was, of course, the special office of the soul friend and may well have been applied beyond the monastic context to those who were seen as being in special need of spiritual support and guidance. There was also a widespread ministry of healing practised both within and beyond the monasteries. The lives of the saints showed it being exercised through healing miracles, blessings and the application of *medicamentia penitentia* as well as plant-based and herbal medicines. Healing was also offered through other less conventional means, including that of poetry. Within the Welsh language there has long been a specific genre of healing poems or *cywydd*. A fine early fifteenth century example from North Wales, written by Guto'r Glyn and addressed to Hywel of Moelrych, a nobleman who had wounded his knee, began:

> I won't sleep much
> Because you're not well.
> My lot is anxiety
> If you're sick.
> If you're healed (God can do it)
> From your wound, I'm fine and very fit.

As well as offering this extreme empathy, the poem went on to invoke the salve of the woman who anointed Jesus in Bethany, and compared Hywel's wife, Elan, to Mary Magdalene, the physician of Jesus, in her capacity to heal her husband. Various plants and remedies were enlisted for their healing potential but ultimately it was poetry itself that was presented as having the greatest efficacy:

> The sound of the poetry of our kinsman Taliesin
> Got his master out of prison.
> I have a mind, because of what I might compose,
> To get the knee out of the prison of a wound.
> Many a person (you're golden-handed)
> Was healed with a *cywydd*.

> I swear by the fire, I too
> Will make an ointment of praise for you.
> And if the mouth (and what it made)
> Doesn't have the power of the medication,
> The host of heaven will make you merrily well.
>
> (Loomis & Johnston 1992: 86)

This extraordinary poem, which takes up the notion of the poet as priest and healer, reads like an elaborate get well card and a statement of empathetic presence through prayer and poetry. The late Donald Allchin, who introduced me to it, reckoned that it reflected a tradition that went back into the golden age of Celtic Christianity. Another very unusual early Celtic poem, rare in its emphasis on the passion of Christ, conveys a somewhat different sense of empathy and presence. Dating from around 760 and attributed to Blathmac, the Irish monk who perished on Iona, slaughtered by the Vikings for refusing to reveal the hiding place of Columba's reliquary with its precious jewels, it portrayed the whole cosmos not just grieving but actually wounding and bleeding with the crucified Christ:

> A stream of blood gushed forth – severe excess!
> So that the bark of every tree was red,
> Here was blood on the breasts of the world,
> In the tree tops of every great forest.

This striking imagery is unlike anything else in the early literature of insular British or Irish Christianity. Its picture of the natural world keening and even bleeding with Jesus on the cross does, however, resonate with the strong sense of empathy displayed in the ministry of pastoral presence practised in the Irish monasteries. It takes us a long way from the stories of the super human saints with their miracles of power and wonder working. Yet that humbler, more wounded and vulnerable dimension is also there in in those stories of Columba and Aidan and in Patrick's *Confessio*. However severe and austere their own lives and faith, they are not simply portrayed as harsh judgmental figures preaching hell fire and dispensing harsh punishments. They were also *anamchairde*, soul friends, buddies, counsellors and to some extent at least fellow travellers and fellow sufferers alongside those whom they comforted and healed through their exercise of a ministry of pastoral presence.

2 PEACE MAKING

Celtic society was fiercely tribal, brutish, militaristic and violent. Celtic Christianity similarly had its macho side, emphasizing manliness and muscular Christianity and lauding monks as the *miles Christi* or soldiers of Christ. But it also offered a counter to this prevailing culture, one based on the precepts of God's kingdom and emphasizing peace, protection and sanctuary. This counter-cultural challenge was clearly expressed in the concept of the monastic compounds not just as sacred enclosures but also as safe spaces and sanctuaries where the values of the kingdom prevailed – peace rather than war, and no violence or abuse. Many people sought shelter and sanctuary in the Celtic monasteries, some fleeing from violence, abuse and oppression and others facing the consequences of their own actions and seeking atonement for their crimes. All were offered protection, justice and healing.

Irish monks were also more actively engaged in peace keeping, none perhaps more so than Adomnán, the ninth abbot of Iona, who seems to have acted as a negotiator and reconciler in various conflicts and to have been instrumental in securing the release of hostages taken captive by the Northumbrian King Ecfrith. In 697 Adomnán formulated *Cáin Adomnáin*, the Law of Adomnán, also known as the Law of the Innocents. It was an attempt to protect non-combatants, specifically women, children and the clergy, in situations of conflict and to give rights to civilians, and especially to women. Adomnán's initiative appears to be one of the first systematic attempts to lessen the savagery of warfare among Christians, a remarkable achievement for a churchman on the remote outer edge of Europe. In it, he gave local expression, in the context of the Gaelic legal tradition, to a wider Christian movement to restrain violence.

The *Cáin Adomnáin* recounted that an angel told Adomnán to create a law that 'women be not in any manner killed by men, through slaughter or any other death, either by poison, or in water, or in fire, or by any other beast, or in a pit, or by dogs, but that they shall die in their lawful bed'. While normally in Irish society crimes against women resulted in fines of only approximately half of those assessed for similar crimes against men, Adomnán's law imposed penalties which were double. It also provided severe sanctions against the killing of children, clerics, clerical students and peasants on clerical lands, rape and impugning the chastity of a noblewoman. It also protected women from having to take part in warfare. Adomnán managed to get the king of Dál Riata, the king of the Picts and more than fifty Irish kings to agree to his Law of the Innocents. It was promulgated at a gathering of 91 Irish, Dál Riatan and Pictish chieftains and clerics at the Synod of Birr in 697. Hailed as one of the first examples of human rights legislation as well as a milestone in the protection of civilians generally and women in particular, it stood as a clear statement against the war-like atmosphere of early mediaeval society in the British Isles. Some have seen its date as significant and suggested that it may have been a centennial celebration of Columba, who had died in 597 and whose Gaelic name Colm Cille, the dove of the church, suggested a commitment to peace.

There were other signs within Celtic Christianity of a commitment to peace. Although the militaristic imagery of Paul's Epistle to the Ephesians was employed in the *lorica* or breastplate prayers, they tended to use the defensive rather than offensive elements, focusing on the shield of faith and helmet of salvation, and not on the sword of the Spirit. The monk who transcribed Matthew's Gospel for the illuminated *Book of Kells*, working most probably in the scriptorium on Iona in the seventh century, changed the Latin word *gladium* to *gaudium* in the 34th verse of Chapter Ten, making Jesus say, 'I came not to send peace, but joy' instead of the more usual 'I came not to send peace, but a sword'. Maybe this was just a mistake, but it is tempting to suggest that he made the alteration because of his unease with the notion of Jesus as sword bearer. If he was indeed wanting to portray Jesus as the bringer of joy then he was expressing a motif that is evident throughout the *Book of Kells*, and which introduces another 'P'- that of play. As Catherine Thom observes in her study of early Irish monasticism, 'Only a fertile and playful imagination would conjure up the illuminations of the *Book of Kells* and similar manuscripts: playfulness seen especially in the vignette of the two rats watched by two cats fighting over the host in the Incarnational Initial, also known as the monogram page' (Thom 2006 :15-16). It is good to be reminded of these elements of playfulness and peace-making alongside the intense austerity and severity that runs through Celtic Christianity.

3 PILGRIMAGE

If I ever had to make a film about early Celtic Christianity I would be tempted to call it 'monks on the move', if not 'nuns on the run'. Pilgrimage, or *peregrinatio* to use the Latin word which they employed, was central to the lives of Irish monks living between the sixth and eighth centuries. They seem for ever to have been on the move, criss-crossing the Irish sea, the Minch, the Bristol Channel and even the English Channel and the North Sea, penetrating deep into Wales, the Scottish mainland, the Inner and Outer Hebrides and many parts of England as well as journeying further afield into Continental Europe where they evangelised and set up monasteries in Belgium, France, Germany and Italy. Irish monks reached as far as the Faroes by 700 and by the end of the eighth century they had reached Iceland. The eighth century *Litany of Pilgrim Saints* chronicled numerous epic journeys, some made in solitude and others in company. To journey over water the monks used curraghs, stout boats ten metres or so long made by stretching up to fifty oak-tanned ox hides over a central wooden rib. On land, they travelled on foot clad in tunics covered by a cowl, carrying a staff, a leather water bottle hanging from their belt and a Gospel book in a leather case slung across their shoulder.

Two of the best known sixth-century Celtic saints, the similarly named, but not to be confused, Columba and Columbanus, were pilgrims *par excellence*, not just in their lives which involved exilic and missionary journeys but also in their approach to faith. Both used the metaphor of pilgrimage to describe the Christian life. Other prominent figures from the golden age of Christianity were also portrayed by their biographers and hagiographers first and foremost as pilgrims. Brendan is perhaps the most obvious example in the famous story of his *Navagatio* from island to island across the Atlantic. Patrick left his British homeland following a call that came to him in a dream to walk as a pilgrim and pastor among the Irish. Fursey, the Irish monk who is credited with evangelising much of East Anglia, was described by Bede as 'a holy man from Ireland, anxious to live the life of a pilgrim for the Lord's sake'. He went on, like Columbanus, to travel through Gaul, establishing a monastery at Lagny near Paris and ending his life as a solitary hermit. Bede also wrote of a Northumbrian monk called Egbert who spent much of his life in Ireland and became imbued with

Irish spiritual values and especially with the call to pilgrimage: 'He would live in exile and never return to his native Britain'. Paulin, who began his monastic life in Wales as a hermit, influenced by St Antony and the desert tradition, travelled to Cornwall where he undertook evangelistic work until, in his biographer's words, 'being on fire with longing for perfection, the idea occurred to him of leaving the land of his fathers where he might live unknown to all save God alone'. He spent his last years as a hermit in Brittany, fasting and leading a life of considerable austerity.

Contemporaries saw a commitment to perpetual pilgrimage, exile and wandering as one of the most striking characteristics of the Irish in the early mediaeval period. 'Why is it', the ninth-century French Benedictine writer Heiric asked, 'that almost the entire population of Ireland, contemptuous of the perils of the sea, has migrated to our shores with a great crowd of teachers? The more learned they are, the more distant their chosen place of exile'. A ninth century monk in St Gall, the Swiss monastery established by Columbanus during his wanderings across Continental Europe, observed that 'wandering is an ineradicable habit of the Irish race'. Historians have concurred with this assessment. In his magisterial modern study of pilgrimage, Jonathan Sumption writes of the early Irish monks:

> Their distinctive contribution to the spiritual life of the 'dark ages' was the idea of the aimless wanderer whose renunciation of the world was the most complete of which man could conceive ... In the wandering Irish hermits of the sixth and seventh centuries, Western Europe came as near as it would ever do to those 'athletes of Christ', the desert fathers of Egypt and Syria in late antiquity. By wandering freely without destination, the Irish hermit felt that he had cut himself off from every material accessory to life.
>
> (Sumption 2002:95-6)

Abbots and others in authority were not always very keen on their monks perpetually wandering around and sometimes tried to put a stop to the practice through which some became *gyrovagues*, itinerant hermits who could not settle anywhere and effectively became tramps. Samthann, a nun, icily responded to a teacher named Dairchellach who expressed the desire to go across the sea on pilgrimage: 'If God could not be found on this side of the sea we would indeed journey across. Since, however, God is nigh unto all who call upon Him, we are under no obligation to cross the sea. The kingdom of Heaven can be reached from every land.' However, no vow of stability was imposed in Irish monasteries, as it was in the later foundations of St Benedict who looked with considerable disfavour on the activities of the wandering *gyrovagues*. Even Columbanus, himself an almost perpetual pilgrim through the last 30 years of his life, was uneasy at the 'aimless wandering' of monks impelled by the call to exile from the world. In a letter to Pope Gregory around 601 he asked what could be done about those who 'for the sake of God and inflamed by the desire for a more perfect life, impugn their vows, leave the place of their first profession, and against their abbot's will, impelled by monastic fervour, either relapse or flee to the deserts'. Despite the concern and strictures of the authorities, there was little that anyone could do to restrain the monks from becoming *peregrini pro Christo*.

It is important to understand what these 'aimless wanderers' understood by pilgrimage. For the Irish monks it was emphatically not about what it became for hundreds of thousands of pilgrims in the later Middle Ages, namely journeying to holy places like Rome or Jerusalem and venerating or touching the relics of saints in order to gain some spiritual benefit or 'buzz'. It was rather a costly form of witness involving perpetual exile from the comforts and distractions of home. Not that they were uninterested in sacred places, as we have already noted (page 59), but the prevailing view in Irish monastic circles about the benefits to be gained from visiting holy sites was profoundly sceptical. It was cogently expressed in a verse attributed to a ninth-century Irish abbot:

> Who to Rome goes
> Much labour, little profit knows;
> For God, on earth though long you've sought him,
> You'll miss in Rome unless you've brought him.

The Irish monks' approach to pilgrimage was based on Biblical teaching, and specifically on God's call to Abraham to leave his home and journey to a strange land and Jesus' words that, while foxes have their holes and the birds of the air their nests, the Son of Man has nowhere to lay his head. It also owed much to the example and teaching of the desert fathers in Egypt and Syria. There is evidence that Egyptian monks journeyed to Ireland – seven are described in an eighth-century manuscript coming to Diseart Uilaig, a site tentatively identified as Dundesert near Crumlin in County Antrim. Irish monks sought their own desert places, often remote and wild like Skellig Michael, a rocky island off the coast of County Kerry, where they established their beehive cells and hermit huts. This is the reason why the words Diseart, Disserth and Dysart are quite often found as place names in Ireland, Wales and Scotland. They indicate early monastic settlements, sometimes just made up of a solitary hermit and in other places constituting a group living a communal life. Irish monks also sought out what they called their places of resurrection where they did penance and prepared for death, rather in the manner of the Hindu *sanyasi*. This practice was not confined to the Celts – four Anglo-Saxon kings went as pilgrims to Rome to die within fifty years in the eighth century – but it seems to have been particularly strong among the Irish. It is reflected in one of the so-called 'hermit poems' from the ninth and tenth centuries: 'Alone in my little hut without a human being in my company, dear has been my pilgrimage before going to meet death'.

Seen in terms of ascetic exile and renunciation of the pleasures and distractions of home and family, *peregrinatio* was a tough calling and costly form of witness to Christ. It was, indeed, at the heart of the much sought after white martyrdom, which involved a life of exile and separation from all that one loved for the sake of God, as well as mortification of the flesh through fasting and penitential exercises. It is worth remembering that in origin the Latin word *peregrinus* meant stranger or outsider and did not necessarily carry connotations of physical journeying. The emphasis in the Latin Christianity of late antiquity, as for example in the theology of Augustine, was on *peregrinatio* involving the separation of Christians from secular life and living apart from others, almost as outcasts, as well as giving up material possessions. Celtic Christians shared this sense of separation from the world, a message which was perhaps reinforced by their attachment to John's Gospel with its strong emphasis on Jesus being shunned by the world. Under the influence of the desert monks of Egypt and Syria, they interpreted it more radically in terms of physical exile and departure from one's homeland, turning *peregrinatio* into a form of pilgrimage.

Penitence was undoubtedly among the main motives which inspired Irish monks to become pilgrims. *Peregrinatio* was undertaken as a way of cleansing the soul through perpetual exile from attachments and distractions and also as a more specific penance to expiate and atone for sins. The Irish penitential system was the first to introduce pilgrimage as a prescribed penance, especially for more serious transgressions such as murder, incest, bestiality and sacrilege. This was later to lead many lay people to go on pilgrimage, but initially it was the monks who embraced it with most alacrity. In some cases, their journeys from their homelands involved serving out a sentence prescribed by the monastic rule or a punishment imposed by the monastic authorities, but often they were undertaken as a voluntary penance, as with those referred to in an eleventh century Irish poem, *The Voyage of the Uí Chorra*:

> We went on our pilgrimage
> At the blast of the whistling wind
> To obtain forgiveness of our sins.
> There is the cause of asking.

A slightly earlier Irish poem, probably dating from the tenth century, further brought out the penitential nature and appeal of pilgrimage:

> A dear pure pilgrimage
> Subduing faults, a body chaste,
> A life of poverty lowly and secluded
> Occur often to my mind.
>
> The gift of piety, the gift of pilgrimage
> The gift of repentance for my soul,
> O Christ without reproach,
> Grant them all to me.

A commitment to mission and evangelism also took monks on pilgrimage and many preached, taught, baptised and buried as they travelled and set up monasteries along the way. Some were undoubtedly motivated too by a sense of adventure and wanderlust. Often, they did know or mind where they were going. An entry in the Anglo-Saxon Chronicle for 891 mentioned three Irish monks who stole away in a boat without oars 'because they desired for the love of God to be in a state of pilgrimage, they cared not whither'. They took enough food for seven days and eventually came ashore on the north coast of Cornwall.

Both penitential and missionary motives seem to have lain behind Columba's departure from Ireland at the age of 41 on the journey that would take him eventually to Iona. He was described by Adomnán simply as sailing away from Ireland to Britain 'wishing to be a pilgrim for Christ'. It is not entirely clear what prompted his departure from Ireland – it may have been penitential, a banishment imposed for some transgression, a voluntary exile or a response to a request from the king of the new Irish colony of Dal Riata in western Scotland. In a popular romantic account which does not surface until the late seventeenth century, Columba was portrayed as stopping off at several islands en route to Iona but moving on when he found that he could still see his beloved Ireland. When he reached Iona, it was only after he had climbed the hill by the bay where he landed and found that he could no longer see Ireland that he decided to stay and found his monastery there. Although the story is almost certainly apocryphal, it underlines the sense of exile and wistful longing felt by the pilgrim who had left his homeland. Whatever his exact motives, Columba was portrayed by hagiographers as the classic *peregrinus pro Christo*. Conjuring up an image that recurs in the lives of many Irish saints of the intrepid pilgrim navigating dangerous seas, Beccan mac Luigdech wrote:

He crossed the wave-strewn wild region, foam-flecked, seal-filled,
   Savage, bounding, seething, white-tipped, pleasing, doleful.

Pilgrimage was not just a dominant theme in Columba's life as chronicled by his hagiographers. It also featured prominently in two of the poems attributed to him. One is quoted at the end of this book; here is the other:

> Alone with none but thee, my God,
> I journey on my way;
> What need I fear when thou art near,
> O King of night and day?
> More safe am I within thy hand,
> Than if a host did round me stand.

A similar emphasis on the Christian life as a way and a journey characterises the writings of Columbanus, perhaps the most travelled of all the Irish pilgrim monks, and certainly the one who reflected most on the theological significance and meaning of pilgrimage. When he was about 45 (much the same age as Columba was when he left Ireland), Columbanus was given permission by Comgall, the abbot of the monastery in Bangor where he was a monk, to go on pilgrimage across Continental Europe. He had been prompted by God's words to Abraham, and according to another more irreverent tradition by the fact that he was being pursued 'by lascivious maidens'. Taking twelve monks with him, he set off from the north east coast of Ireland, travelled down the western seaboard of Britain, crossed Cornwall and travelled through France, founding monasteries at Annegray, Luxeuil and Fontaine in the Vosges region. He and his companions fell out with both the ecclesiastical authorities and the local rulers and were forcibly marched under guard to Nantes to be sent back to Ireland. However, a storm blew the ship that was to return them aground at the mouth of the Loire and the captain, taking this as a sign that God did not approve of their expulsion, allowed them to go free. They wandered across northern France, rowed up the Rhine and eventually came to Bregenz on Lake Constance in Switzerland. There one of the monks, Gall, remained to found a monastery while Columbanus and the others crossed over the Alps into Lombardy. He founded his final monastery at Bobbio between Genoa and Piacenza and died there in 615, thirty years after leaving Ireland.

Columbanus' monastic rule was taken up by over 60 monasteries in France, Belgium and Switzerland which were founded by his followers. Although he became something of a cult figure and was much sought out for his counsel and spiritual wisdom, he remained a solitary ascetic and spent much of his time in caves living off wild apples and herbs. He fell foul of bishops who found it hard to come to terms with the activities of this restless individual who insisted he was first and last a pilgrim for Christ. Columbanus spoke of pilgrims as '*hospes mundi*', or guests of the world, a phrase which epitomised the ambivalence of pilgrimage, at once an austere, penitential calling and a somewhat self-indulgent and parasitic lifestyle relying on other people's generosity and living off their hospitality.

Columbanus' sermons kept returning to the theme of human life as a pilgrimage and show how his thirty years of exile and wandering coloured his own theology:

We who are on the road should hasten on, for the whole of our life is like one day's journey. Just like pilgrims we should continuously sigh for and long for our homeland, for travellers are always filled with hope and desire for the road's end. And so, since we are travellers and pilgrims in this world, let us think upon the end of the road, that is of our life, for the end of our way is our home.

(Walker 1957:97)

There are other examples in early mediaeval Celtic Christian sources of the central importance of pilgrimage as a metaphor for Christian life. Whatever its purpose and provenance, and the prevailing view among current scholars is that it should be read as an allegory of the monastic life, the *Navigatio Sancti Brendani* gives a wonderful sense of the adventure of pilgrimage and stands as one of the great classics of the literature of travel and journeying. The Irish Penitentials also emphasized the theme of pilgrimage, not just by prescribing it for the first time in Western Christianity as a penance for those found guilty of some transgression but also through their whole approach to the continuum of sin, repentance and forgiveness. In his important study of them Hugh Connolly describes their 'pilgrimage model' of penance as 'quintessentially Celtic':

All of life is seen as a form of pilgrimage. It is precisely along this life path that each Christian must make his pilgrim's progress ... . Recognizing that every Christian must, in some sense, experience a 'wandering in the desert' before attaining 'the promised land', it becomes apparent that he must be equipped mentally and spiritually to survive the desert ordeal.

The symbols of Celtic Christianity, whilst at times harsh and severe, had the merit of reminding each Christian that they had to make their own journey. Thus life was focussed, life was purposed. In journeying toward Christ, Christians also journeyed deeper into themselves and began to forge their personal moral identity.

(Connolly 1995:177-8;201)

It was pointed out to me during a course which I led on Celtic Christianity at the Gladstone Library in North Wales in 2015 how very male-oriented this Celtic view of pilgrimage was. Women, for the most part, were not able to engage in the kind of perpetual peregrination and wandering that characterised the lives of so many male monks. They were tied to domestic duties, to home and to children. For those female saints who were portrayed as leaving home, the motivation was often not *wanderlust*, desire to follow Christ or to do penance but rather escape from abuse, violence and personal danger. This was certainly the case with the three best known female Welsh saints, Non, Melangell and Winifred, all of whom were portrayed as fleeing from unwelcome male attentions, in two cases having been the victims of rape. For them, and probably for many other saintly women, pilgrimage, if indeed we can call it by that name, was not about the intentional heroic sacrifice of white or green martyrdom but a much more basic matter of seeking their own safety in a desperate situation. It is a further reminder of how very male-dominated the world of Celtic Christianity was, certainly as it has come down to us from the early sources, and how little we know about that largely hidden female side of it.

In time, the Celtic pilgrim tradition developed more along the lines found in the Irish Penitentials and the writings of Columbanus and became more focussed on the inner pilgrimage of faith rather than the outward business of physical journeying and wandering. There was a growing realisation that the pilgrim path of renunciation and asceticism could be pursued without gadding around the world. Some centuries after their deaths the pioneer Celtic saints came to inspire pilgrimages of precisely the kind for which they themselves had had no time. Almost as much as Rome and Jerusalem, Celtic Christian sites like Iona, Croagh Patrick, St David's and Lindisfarne became places of pilgrimage, as people sought contact with the holy men and women whose saintly lives were being written up by hagiographers in ever more fanciful and effusive ways from the ninth century onwards. Across Europe as a whole, the cult of saints and relics was about to usher in the golden age of Christian pilgrimage and take it far away from the lonely and austere lives of exile practised by the Irish monks. Ironically their own promotion of pilgrimage as a penitential exercise paved the way for its widespread popularity and take-up, but it was a very different kind of peregrination from the radical exile and white martyrdom that they had practised.

8
Some missing Ps - what we don't find in Celtic Christianity

After highlighting some of the dominant themes in Celtic Christianity, I feel it may also be useful to mention very briefly some significant doctrines which are conspicuously absent in the main sources.

1 Passion
Christ's passion is curiously neglected in virtually all the main sources from Celtic Christianity's golden age. As I have already noted, there is an overwhelming emphasis on creation and much about judgement and the Second Coming but very little indeed about the suffering and passion of Jesus, or its atoning significance. It is the symbol of the triumphant Christ, or *Christus Victor*, which is found overwhelmingly on the high standing crosses. By contrast, later Mediaeval Irish and Scottish crosses are much more likely to display prominent images of the naked Jesus hanging in agony on the cross.

2 Patripassianism
There is no indication of the doctrine which is known as divine passibility or patripassianism (the idea that God suffers). The literary sources for Celtic Christianity convey a strong sense of divine power and impassibility and very little sense indeed of God's suffering. There is no anticipation at all of the theology of patripassianism developed in the later twentieth century, notably by the Reformed theologian Jürgen Moltmann in his classic work *The Crucified God*.

3 Predestination
I can find no hint of the doctrine of double predestination in any of the literary sources from the golden age of Celtic Christianity. Eurigena specifically set out to refute the teaching of Gottschalk

and Augustine that some souls were predestined to heaven and others to hell. Pelagius' emphasis on free will and the importance of practical good works can be seen as being in fundamental opposition to a doctrine of double predestination, as can the more general Celtic Christian emphasis on puritanical perfectionism with its implication that how lives are lived is more important than God's preordained plan in the attainment of salvation.

This is not to say that Celtic Christians were without a sense of God's providence and divine destiny and decree. The second verse of the poem attributed to Columba and quoted on page 130 begins 'My destined time is fixed by Thee, and death does know its hour'.

4 Purgatory

I find myself in total agreement with the assessment of the Breton Benedictine scholar Louis Gougaud who wrote 85 years ago in his classic study of *Christianity in Celtic Lands* that 'in the Irish writings previous to the tenth century which have reached us, whether theological treatises, narratives of visions of the state after death, or works of any other description, we come across nothing to attest the belief in a Purgatory distinct from Hell. The word (*purgatorium*, or, in Irish, *purgatoir*) – as well as the idea – does not appear till later in religious literature.' (Gougaud 1992:294)

5 Penal substitution

There is no hint of the theory of atonement known as penal substitution in any of the writings from the golden age of Celtic Christianity. Although there is a good deal about divine judgement, there is relatively little about the doctrine of atonement and certainly no suggestion of substitutionary atonement, whereby Jesus' death is interpreted as a punishment in the place of sinners to satisfy the demands of an angry and judging God.

6 Pauline theology

The overwhelming Biblical influences on the poems, prayers, liturgies and other texts which have survived from the golden age of Celtic Christianity are the Psalms and the Gospels. It is much more difficult to detect any influence from the epistles of St Paul with their particular Christological focus and their emphasis on the contrast between law and grace and justification by faith alone. It is true that the early Irish *lorica*, or breastplate prayers and poems, clearly draw on imagery in Ephesians 6:11-20 but there is much uncertainty among New Testament scholars as to whether this epistle was, in fact, the work of Paul.

7 Pride

This last 'P' is not so much a missing element in Celtic Christianity but rather the condition which is most reviled and repudiated. For all the puritanical perfectionism and spiritual élitism that undoubtedly prevailed in Irish monasticism, there was universal agreement that pride, and especially spiritual pride, was the greatest and most deadly of all sins. In the words of Fursey, 'the cause and root of all evil is pride' (Rackham 2007:37).

Part 3

Following the Way Today

9
Following the Celtic Way today

The Celtic way as I have outlined it in this book is not quite as appealing as the version I presented 25 years ago. However, there are still several features that provide food for thought and perhaps even models for those seeking to live out their Christian lives today. It may indeed be that some of its less immediately attractive features actually have a heightened relevance in our troubled and uncertain times. This last chapter will explore how contemporary Christians might follow the Celtic way.

In one crucial respect many Christians, especially younger ones, are already following the Celtic way quite unconsciously. Although I have not highlighted it especially in this book, it was not a denominational or confessional way in the sense that post-Reformation Christianity has largely been until recently. As I pointed out on page 21, it is a mistake to read Celtic Christianity as a branch of the church like Catholicism, Protestantism or Orthodoxy and even more erroneous to view 'the Celtic church' as a self-conscious denomination like the Church of England or the Methodists. Indigenous insular Celtic-speaking Christians in the British Isles in the early middle ages had no concept of belonging to a particular denomination or a distinct and self-contained church. They had an outlook that was both universal, in terms of the overriding allegiance to the Trinitarian God, and very local in terms of their rootedness in tribe, kin group and monastery. We are today moving into a post-denominational Christianity where old denominational identities and loyalties mean less and less, especially to young people. In this respect, many are indeed already on the Celtic way.

As I have pointed out again and again in this book, Celtic Christianity, especially as it is presented in the sources which have come down to us from its perceived golden age, was essentially a monastic phenomenon. The stories and lives of the saints and the early poems and prayers, just as much as the rules and

Penitentials, came out of monasteries and have monastic life as their primary subject matter and focus. There is much interest today in monasticism and a whole new movement in contemporary Christianity goes under the name of 'the new monasticism'. As conventional churchgoing and church membership decline steeply, more and more Christians see themselves as 'resident aliens' to use the phrase coined by Stanley Hauerwas, living counter-cultural lives in increasingly secular societies. Such an attitude encourages thoughts of monastic style intentional communities, or 'colonies of heaven' as I called them in an earlier book, functioning somewhat like the Celtic monasteries in a largely pagan Britain.

Several writers have seen the future of Christianity as lying largely with the development of such monastic style communities. Dietrich Bonhoeffer famously wrote as long ago as 1935 that 'the restoration of the church will surely come only from a new type of monasticism ... I think it is time to gather people together to do this'. In his seminal work *After Virtue*, published in 1981, the Scottish moral philosopher Alistair MacIntyre drew on the example of the resilience of monasteries in the so-called dark ages to suggest that in 'the new dark ages which are already upon us.... what matters is the construction of local forms of community within which civility and the intellectual and moral life can be sustained'. More recently, the American journalist and blogger, Rod Dreher, whose own spiritual journey has taken him from Methodism via Catholicism to the Orthodox church, in his best-selling book *The Benedict Option* (2017) has argued that in a society which is no longer Christian, those who do still adhere to the faith should distance themselves from the world and creates new communities. His particular model for these is Benedictine monasticism.

As we have seen, dispersed communities following a rule of life and shared disciplines have been one of the most practical fruits of the current Celtic Christian revival. There are aspects of Celtic monasticism which we would not want to return to or emulate today – the spiritual élitism and hierarchy, the extreme asceticism and puritanical perfectionism, for example. But there are others which might provide a model for the future of the church – the regular discipline of prayer as a bedrock, the collegiality and mutual support of an intentional community, the ministry of pastoral presence and hospitality. In my book *Colonies of Heaven* I suggested that the approach to ministry modelled in the Celtic monasteries might offer a future for the church in place of the parish church model which has served us well for thousand years or so but which is now visibly collapsing and no longer viable. We do not necessarily need to think in terms of residential communities and we certainly do not want to create new institutions which are cut off from the world by metaphorical or physical walls. The Celtic monasteries were very much in if not wholly of the world, colonies of heaven which pointed to the values of Christ's kingdom while being rooted in their local environments and cultures, preserving popular traditions and serving people's needs. Maybe they are worth considering as we ponder where the future of Christian witness and service lies.

There is one subject which I feel bound to mention in this context, if only because it has received so much publicity in recent decades. The child abuse scandals that have so rocked the church have been particularly associated with monasteries and other closed and somewhat secretive institutions. There is no evidence that abuse took place in Celtic monasteries where young boys were regularly fostered out to live with and be taught by monks. Given the weakness and frailty of human nature, however, it may have occurred. Nowadays, when we are so much more conscious of the potential dangers inherent in such situations and communities, we need to make sure as far as possible that modern monasteries of whatever kind are fully open and accountable and unable to harbour and cover up abusive relationships.

The rhythm of prayer which lies at the heart of monasticism is certainly something which a growing number of Christians are re-discovering and applying in their own lives today. Daily prayer is becoming more popular at both an individual and corporate level with more churches holding daily services. The psalms are also being recovered and more use is being made of them in both public worship and private devotion. I myself have turned increasingly to the psalms of lament in our recent troubled times. They are among the passages in the Bible which speak most clearly of the absence of God and where desperate pleas for help and protection seem to go unheeded and unanswered. This is the experience of many people today, as I know when I have written and preached on this topic. Re-discovering the psalms, and especially those which express lament and anger as well as praise and thankfulness, perhaps enables us to find a way of conveying our sense of God's absence and distance which is still very much within the Judeo-Christian Biblical tradition.

Poetry also has an increasing place in contemporary spirituality and worship. I am conscious of more and more preachers and worship leaders who use poems in their sermons and services. The modern Celtic Christian revival has undoubtedly played a part in making church worship less leaden and prosy and giving it a more poetic and rhythmic quality. As attention spans shorten, especially among young people accustomed to tweets and twitter, the appealing, arresting imagery and rhythmic brevity of a poetic approach to worship is going to become ever more important. So, too, is the physical dimension which was so prominent in the witness and worship of the Irish monks. I am not suggesting that Christians start resorting to multiple genuflections and prostrations, or take up the practice of standing for hours up to their waists or necks in cold water. But there is already a movement to engage the body in worship as well as the mind and spirit, not least through drama, dance and mime, processions and pilgrimages. It is important to preserve the sense of balance that was so important in Celtic monastic life. We should remember its three cardinal principles of prayer, manual work and focussed intellectual study and meditation. Our worship in western Christianity may have become over-cerebral and may need to become more embodied but that does not mean throwing the baby out with the bathwater and abandoning its rational and intellectual aspects. We worship, praise and glorify God with our minds, our bodies and our spirits and all three need to be nurtured, sustained and challenged in a healthy Christian life.

Provisionality is certainly a theme well worth the contemporary church pondering. Much time and energy nowadays is expended in trying to maintain and repair the fabric of old church buildings which were erected at a time when there were more churchgoers and when the prevailing norm was what I have categorized as the Roman or Norman model of building grandiose and solid temples designed to last for hundreds of years (pages 62 – 3). In our very different circumstances now, it is perhaps time to return to the Celtic model of provisionality. Once again, it is important to maintain a sense of balance here. There is evidence that traditional and beautiful old church buildings, especially cathedrals, are attracting young people in particular to the Christian faith. Attendance at cathedral services is indeed bucking the trend of general decline in churchgoing among the mainstream denominations. Where practical and feasible it is certainly desirable to maintain and keep open beautiful old churches which can preach sermons in stone and draw people to ponder the mysteries of faith. I have argued elsewhere that they may well be able to fulfil this role better when they are quiet and empty than when they are filled with the noise and busyness of worship. But the era of building massive and magnificent new churches has surely come to an end. There is almost certainly room for more multi-purpose buildings where worship can be combined with social and community use. There is also a case for returning to the provisionality and flexibility of Celtic Christianity, with its sense of the impermanence and temporariness of all human structures and its understanding of the church as a movement and journey rather than a static institution.

The patterned lives and attitudes which I have suggested characterized Celtic Christianity certainly have much to teach us. They point to the importance of balance and rhythm and also to the role that art and imagination can play in the expression of faith. We do indeed need to follow Jesus' teaching as rendered in *The Message* and 'learn the unforced rhythms of grace'. Techniques of mindfulness and meditation, with their focus on breathing out and breathing in, can help here as can the cultivation of the kind of balanced life suggested in the *Alphabet of Devotion* (page 65).

The Celtic Christian understanding of God, as outlined in Chapter 5 of this book, perhaps immediately offers fewer obvious pathways for contemporary Christians to follow. Certainly, those of us on the more liberal wing of the church would want to emphasize divine vulnerability and patripassianism as much as the primordial aspects of an omnipotent and distant deity. We would also want to affirm God's gentleness rather than his role as a stern judge. Maybe this is just wishful thinking and certainly I have found that reading the really rather forbidding theological utterances of the early Celtic Christians has challenged my own view of God, although it has not changed it. The emphasis on God's protective powers is certainly highly relevant to those who find themselves in situations of danger, depression and abuse of any kind. As I myself discovered during a period as a psychiatric hospital chaplain, simple prayers of protection based on the *lorica* model seem to speak powerfully and helpfully to those leading disordered, frightening and chaotic lives, and especially to those suffering from schizophrenia and depression. It may well be that in our present somewhat disturbed and uncertain times, when many are feeling anxious and depressed, assurance of God's power, presence and protection is especially needed and the Celtic Christian emphasis on these particular divine attributes may perhaps resonate more than it did in the rather happier and more carefree era when *The Celtic Way* was written.

The notion of pleroma, applied both to God and to God's creation, is one which does have much appeal and relevance today, I think. It encourages notions of pluralism and diversity both within the Godhead, with the doctrine of the Trinity suggesting relationality and *perichoresis*, or interpenetration and mutual exchange, between the three persons of Father/Creator, Son/Redeemer and Holy Spirit/Sustainer, and across the whole of creation. I have explored a theology of diversity, based in part on the idea of pleroma, in Chapter 6 of my book *Grace, Order, Openness and Diversity* (2010). Specifically, taking on board the idea of pleroma commits us to ecological concern and environmental activism. Once we really grasp the notion of the fullness and rich diversity of God's creation and the significance of every part of it, then we can surely no longer go on destroying species, cutting down tropical rain forests, contributing to climate change or turning the good earth into dust bowls and deserts. In this respect at least, Celtic Christianity does seem to me to have a clear environmental message, even if it is not as explicitly 'green' and nature-friendly as some of its more enthusiastic proponents have suggested.

In terms of our human responses to God, penitence is perhaps simultaneously the least appealing but also potentially one of the more important themes in Celtic Christianity worth pondering today. Nowadays, when there is much less fear of Hell and judgement than in the early Middle Ages, it may seem unduly gloomy and even masochistic to focus so much on our unworthiness and sinfulness. However, there may be benefits in returning to the early Irish way of encouraging an attitude of genuine contrition and practising both penitence and penance, understood in the context of healing, and accompanied by a soul friend. Many of us carry around burdens of self-imposed guilt and stress. Discovering ways to free ourselves and let go of these debilitating burdens, find assurance of forgiveness and move on in our lives can be hugely helpful to our mental, physical and spiritual health. It may actually help to start, as Patrick did in his *Confessio*, by acknowledging our own sinfulness and lack of belief and throwing ourselves on God's ever-present and unlimited mercy.

There is a growing consensus in those churches which practise it that the whole business of confession should be mutual rather than mechanical. The modern Roman Catholic Church prefers the term reconciliation to confession and emphasises the mutuality and the elements of on-going healing and pilgrimage present in the early Irish penitential tradition. Old style dark confessional boxes, with their reinforcement of a sense of separation between priest and penitent, are increasingly being replaced by face-to-face meetings and discussions. A significant sense of mutuality is embodied in the two-way prayer of confession found in the liturgy of the Iona Community, where the worship leader first confesses her or his own failings to the rest of the worshipping group, who respond with words confirming God's absolution and forgiveness, before themselves confessing and receiving a similar assurance from the worship leader. The idea of the soul friend has been taken up and championed both in communities like that of Aidan and Hilda and also in contemporary pastoral care and pastoral theology. Its relevance and possible application today is well explored in such books as Kenneth Leech's *Soul Friend: A Study of Spirituality* (1977, revised edition, 1994) and Ray Simpson's *Soul Friendship: Celtic Insights into Spiritual Mentoring* (1999).

Praise is perhaps a more tricky area. On the face of it, we can never praise God enough and the Celtic Christian attitude of constant praise, both at an individual and corporate level, is surely to be commended and emulated. Yet are some contemporary churches too fixated on praise, with an unvaried diet of worship songs led by praise bands which focus on just one aspect of the human relationship with and response to God without any acknowledgement of those other feelings of lament, anger, yearning and hope which are found in the Psalms? There is surely a danger in shallow praise which does not fully express and engage with genuine more negative human emotions. God is surely big enough to take all our feelings on board. Having said this, there is certainly room for more blessing in our society where so many suffer low self-esteem and feel unrecognised and unrewarded. The ministry of benediction, exercised both by individuals and by the church corporately in the name of Christ, speaking well of people and of the world, is one that we would do well to cultivate and extend following the example of the Celtic saints. There may, too, be a place for cursing although I suspect there is more than enough of that in our world.

The call to poverty is, of course, a key theme of Jesus' teaching. Indeed, he has much more to say on that subject than he does on the matter of sexuality although you would never guess this from the issues and debates currently obsessing most churches. His clear message that the way to enter the kingdom of heaven is to give away all that we have to the poor remains a very challenging one which I for one have failed to heed. I certainly cannot say in all conscience, as the author of 'Be thou my vision' does, 'riches I heed not, nor man's empty praise'. Spiritual poverty is perhaps as important and as difficult to cultivate as material poverty. There is much to meditate and reflect on in Jesus' words 'Blessed are the poor in spirit' with their commendation of the unassuming and humble. Spiritual pride, rightly singled out by Celtic Christians as a particularly deadly sin, remains a terrible temptation today.

Prophecy is a difficult subject to address for those of us who are not charismatics. It may well be that some Christians do possess that gift and should exercise it although there are also pitfalls and abuses to be wary of here. The other aspect of prophetic ministry as practised by the Celtic saints, speaking truth to power and counselling, upbraiding and challenging those in authority, is certainly important and is well understood by many churches and Christian groups today who feel compelled by Gospel imperatives to critique Government policies, draw attention to injustices and call rulers to account. The model of Aidan remains inspiring in this respect and that is one of the reasons why I have proposed him for the vacant post of patron saint of the United Kingdom (Bradley 2007:211).

Patience and perseverance remain key Christian virtues which, like so many others, are easier to write about than to put into practice. Waiting is an inescapable part of the human condition and a state that we all find ourselves in at various times of our lives. Indeed, we all do a lot of waiting – and it is often a time of anxiety and stress, waiting for an overdue bus or train, a phone call that we fear may bring bad news, a hospital appointment or results of blood test, an exam or a job interview. We often feel at our most vulnerable and helpless when we are waiting. In a classic work of twentieth century Christian devotional literature, *The Stature of Waiting*, William Vanstone argued that it is when we are in the state of waiting for something or someone outside our control that we are closest to Christ. The divine image that we bear then is one of passive suffering, of waiting and letting things be done to us, as they were to Jesus in his passion. Vanstone suggested that those immobilized by strokes or hooked up to life-support machines, along with those facing unemployment, depression or dementia, share in some way in what Jesus experienced when he was handed over by Pontius Pilate to be crucified – a switch from active to passive living where life becomes a matter of waiting on the decisions and initiatives of others and on external events over which we have no control. Yet it was precisely when he was experiencing the 'stature of waiting' that Jesus was closest to God and achieved his costly work as saviour of the world. We, too, can find ourselves, voluntarily or involuntarily, in a similar 'stature of waiting' where all our resources of patience and perseverance will be needed.

Practical action is very much on the agenda of most churches and Christian denominations today. There is a growing realisation that commitment to the Gospel means walking the walk as well as talking the talk, following Jesus' well-known but unfailingly challenging words at the end of the parable of the sheep and goats in Matthew 25.40 that 'in as much as you did it to the least of my brethren you did it to me', and getting stuck into practical social projects and community action. Churches have been disproportionately active in the setting up of refuges, drop-in centres and food banks, often on an inter-denominational basis and in co-operation with other agencies. The calls to good works and practical action found in the sermons and the writings of Pelagius quoted on pages 116 – 17 remain very relevant if challenging reading.

In many ways these practical initiatives embody the notion of the ministry of presence as outlined in the first section of Chapter 7. I want to reiterate what I first said in my book on Columba more than 20 years ago:

> The notion of pastoral presence is one that could fruitfully be made much more of by contemporary Christians. It seems

to me to provide a helpful ecclesiological model for churches struggling to find a role and identity. We are obsessed with the model of mission nowadays with churches forever being encouraged to undertake a mission audit, produce mission action plans and train congregations as missionary cells. This is essentially managerial jargon – witness how no business nowadays seems to be able to operate without a mission statement –and in the words of a perceptive religious commentator, Clifford Longley, 'managerial jargon will not stir our lost sea of faith'.

(Bradley 1996:115)

I went on to quote the words of Gillean Craig, an Anglican priest ministering in Central London, arguing for the development of a theology of witness as opposed to a theology of mission. Witness, as we have discovered, was a hugely important concept and model for Celtic Christians and it expresses very strongly the idea of pastoral presence which was also at the heart of their understanding of the Christian calling. His words, which first appeared in an article in the *Church Times* on 2 February 1996, are worth quoting again here:

Witnesses are not people radically different from those to whom they witness. Witnesses are people whose experience gives them a story to tell that confronts others with, and helps them to come to a decision about, the truth. Our witnessing can take a wide range of authentic forms, depending on our circumstances, talents and abilities. It ranges from the constant and steady witness of the faithful presence – the people ready to suffer and rejoice with their neighbours, the church still open for prayers and praise – to the dynamism of radical social action, of open-air evangelism and challenging drama. We can be mute witnesses in the holiness of our lives, and vocal witnesses telling others the story of Christ. There is a whole theology of witness to explore.

The practical working out of such a theology of witness and of a ministry of pastoral presence was demonstrated very clearly in the response and role of local churches in North Kensington in the aftermath of the terrible fire which devastated Grenfell Tower in June 2017. St Clement's, the local parish church just two hundred yards away from the stricken tower block, opened its doors to the sulphurous night air at 3am while the fire was still raging and around 200 people gathered there, including traumatised survivors and others evacuated from neighbouring high-rise blocks. Other churches in the vicinity subsequently opened their doors to provide places of safety and refuge, prayer and counselling and practical necessities like food, water, clothes and nappies. They also became hubs and shrines for grieving local people. In the words of Graham Tomlin, the Bishop of Kensington, 'our most important contribution was just being there. We were present when people were going through the most horrendous time and it was appreciated. In the aftermath of the fire, people connected with the church'. (*The Times* 15 July 2017)

There are many other examples of a ministry of presence being exercised in the contemporary church. One very far removed from the noise and chaos of inner-city London is the healing centre established beside the tiny church of Pennant Melangell in mid-Wales. This remote church, accessed via a long single lane road between high hedges, contains a highly unusual shrine erected in the twelfth century to house the relics of the seventh-century female Celtic saint Melangell, famous for sheltering a hare fleeing from a hunting expedition led by a Welsh prince. During her ministry there in the late 1980s and early 1990s, Evelyn Davies established Pennant Melangell as a place of support, counselling and healing for those suffering from terminal cancer and their carers. Many other initiatives by churches across the country have been inspired by a similar commitment to a ministry of quiet and faithful pastoral presence. In a society such as ours where so much is short-term and fast moving, the notion of presence and of being there for the long haul is almost counter-cultural. The ministry of pastoral presence is demanding but it is also hugely needed. It ties in both with the Celtic figure of the soul friend and also with the modern nostrum of mindfulness, in terms of being present in ourselves and also in giving our attention to those around us. Writing about practical pastoral care based on her experiences as medical director of a hospice, Sheila Cassidy commends 'the friend who walks alongside, helping, sharing and sometimes just sitting, empty-handed, when he would rather run away. It is a spirituality of *presence*, of being alongside, watchful, available; of being *there*'. (Cassidy 2002:5)

The need for peace-keeping and reconciliation work is as great as ever in a world which seems frighteningly divided and violent.

Again, there are many impressive contemporary examples of this particular expression of Christian commitment. Christian Peacemaker Teams work in Palestine, Colombia and Iraqi Kurdistan seeking to reduce violence and defuse tensions by unarmed intervention and non-violent action. Those involved in these teams are ready to risk injury or death through their presence in crisis situations and militarized areas at the invitation of local peace and human rights workers. Another initiative which perhaps has even closer affiliations with the role played by Irish monasteries is the development in the United States of sanctuary churches where immigrants are specifically welcome and anti-immigrant laws passed by the Trump Administration do not prevail.

Pilgrimage remains for me both the most distinctive and emphasized feature of Celtic Christianity and also the one with most contemporary resonances and relevance. Growing interest and participation in pilgrimage has been one of the most striking aspects of the spiritual landscape of Europe over recent decades. I have written about it in my book *Pilgrimage: A Spiritual and Cultural Journey* (2009). Old pilgrim routes have been revived and there has been a plethora of new pilgrim ways established across the continent. Within the British Isles, many of these have drawn on the appeal of Celtic saints and Celtic Christian sites. They include St Cuthbert's Way linking Melrose and Lindisfarne; the Two Saints Way between Chester and Lichfield; the Saints' Way crossing mid-Cornwall from coast to coast; the Bishop's Road from Llawhaden to St David's in Pembrokeshire; the pilgrim way through North Wales and down the Llyn Peninsula to Bardsey island; the Saints Road on the Dingle Peninsula in county Kerry; the *Tochar Phadraig* from Balintubber Abbey to the summit of Croagh Patrick in county Mayo; the Whithorn Way from Glasgow to St Ninian's cave at Whithorn; and the *Slí Cholmcille* or St Columba trail from Donegal to Iona. Places associated with the golden age of Celtic Christianity have become magnets for tourists, many of whom describe themselves as pilgrims. Lindisfarne, where Aidan and Cuthbert ministered, receives around 650,000 visitors a year and Iona, where Columba established his monastic base, nearly 250,000. Irish monastic sites like Glendalough, Clonmacnoise, Kells and Monasterboice are also hugely popular.

On the face of it, this kind of modern pilgrimage is very different indeed from the *peregrinatio* practised by the Irish monks.

It is about travelling to holy places, often in the comfort of cars, trains or luxury coaches, and getting a spiritual buzz from visiting them rather than about experiencing the perpetual sense of exile and wandering that so animated the Irish monks and about which Columbanus wrote so powerfully.

Yet in several respects contemporary movements within Christianity do echo the Celtic theme of *peregrinatio*. It chimes in with the way that increasing numbers of people see their faith. Surveys suggest that far more Christians now than in previous generations describe their faith as an on-going journey rather than as a sudden decisive conversion experience. The road to Emmaus, along which the resurrected Jesus travelled with two of his disciples for many miles before they recognised him, seems to resonate with more believers nowadays than the road to Damascus where Paul underwent a sudden blinding conversion. Pilgrimage has much to offer an age such as ours where there is so much anxiety, yearning and seeking. It fits the needs of a restless generation – but perhaps restlessness is, in fact, part and parcel of the human condition. Bruce Chatwin, the travel writer, has suggested in his book *Songlines* that humans are born to be nomads and that our natural inclinations turn us to movement and journeying.

There is a clear contemporary attraction to the idea of provisionality implicit in the Celtic Christian attachment to *peregrinatio*. Especially among young Christians, denominational ties are loosening and there is a movement away from authority, institutional structures and hierarchies in favour of a vision of the church as an on-going movement and community which is not static or hidebound. Rejecting what they see as outmoded and unnecessary ecclesiastical barriers and encumbrances, many today would echo Jean Vanier's dictum that 'a sect has control at its heart, a community has journey at its heart'.

Alongside these more metaphorical connections, the actual physical pilgrimages made by more and more Christians nowadays also resonate with themes in Celtic Christianity. For a start, they do often manifest an embodied physical spirituality. Increasingly, people are walking or cycling pilgrim ways. This development ties in with concern about the environment and also with promoting fitness and combatting obesity. Modern pilgrims may not subject themselves to quite as much severe and rigorous austerity as the early Irish monks but they are similarly modelling an approach to faith which is physical as well as intellectual and active as well as passive. There is a growing interest in walking as well as talking the faith. As fewer people are prepared to sit passively in churches on a Sunday morning being preached at, more are happy to go on prayer walks, use labyrinths and undertake pilgrimages. This trend has been especially noticeable in Scandinavia where the lowest level of church attendance in Europe is accompanied by a booming interest in pilgrimage, the development of a specialist ministry of pilgrim pastors and the working out of a whole practical theology of pilgrimage.

The contemporary growth in pilgrimage offers many opportunities for churches. Perhaps the greatest is to help tourists become pilgrims. The dividing line between pilgrims and tourists has long been blurred and is becoming increasingly more so. It has been said that while tourists pass through a particular place, for pilgrims that place passes through them. With the development of enriched and specifically faith focused tourism, the latter experience is perhaps becoming more common. It is also said that while tourists return from their travels with souvenirs, pilgrims come back with blessings and with their lives somehow changed. Yet pilgrims have long returned home with souvenirs and many camera-toting and coach-borne visitors to churches and sacred places pause to light a candle and pray. If some of what passes for pilgrimage today is really tourism, it is also the case that many modern tourists are searching for something beyond a holiday. I firmly believe that one of our greatest callings and opportunities as Christians and in churches today is to help tourists become pilgrims. Nowhere is this happening more than in those 'thin' Celtic places like Iona where the boundaries between tourism and pilgrimage and more generally between the sacred and the secular are especially porous and thin.

There is much enthusiasm for recovering the notion prevalent in the early church of Christians as followers of the Way. This can have many different dimensions. It may mean leading more intentional lives, perhaps in dispersed communities following a prescribed rule of life. It may mean sitting more loosely to structures and hierarchies, being more inclusive, more open to new ideas and more prepared to take risks. Many Christians now involve themselves in protest vigils, walks, marches and demonstrations for peace and justice, sponsored swims, walks and cycle rides. Perhaps these are the new pilgrimages for our age, often carried out alongside those of other faiths and those of no faith. For Christians, the way will always involve following the one who had nowhere to lay his head and carried out his peripatetic ministry, teaching, preaching and healing as he journeyed along.

Particular emphases which we find within the Celtic Christian approach can help us in our own contemporary pilgrimages. There is the balance between *peregrinatio* and presence. On the face of it, these seem conflicting values, the one emphasizing movement, restless journeying and perpetual wandering, and the other stability, steady availability and being there for others. Yet although there is undoubtedly an ambiguity and tension here, these two very different attitudes and approaches to life were held together by the Irish monks. We come back here to the importance of rhythm and balance, to the unforced rhythms of God's grace. Perhaps most important in this context was the Celtic Christian emphasis on the significance of the return journey in pilgrimage which was seen as every bit as valuable as the outward one. As we have noted, Columbanus preached that 'every day you depart and every day you return; you depart in returning and you return in departing, different ending, same beginning.' Eurigena similarly held that all things proceed out of God and are destined to return into him. The principle that everything and everyone returned back to their source in God was particularly important to him. He found it strongly confirmed in the opening verses of the Book of Ecclesiastes where there is a sense that for all the apparent vanity and futility of life there is a pattern with the sun and wind returning to the place where they arose and the rivers running back into the sea which is never full. As he put it. 'gyring in a gyre the Spirit goes forth and then comes back to its own place'.

In pilgrimage, the journey back is as important as the outward journey or the destination. We arrive only to depart again and coming home is as significant as setting out. The pilgrim comes back changed and hopefully more open as well as more faithful than before. The late eighteenth century French writer Chateaubriand maintained that 'there was never a pilgrim that did not come back to his own village with one less prejudice and one more idea'. The twentieth century Welsh poet and priest, R.S.Thomas, expressed the central purpose of pilgrimage thus in his poem 'Somewhere':

The point of travelling is not
To arrive but to return home
Laden with pollen you shall work up
Into honey the mind feeds on.

So many of our experiences in life can be seen in terms of the importance of returning home – the return from our daily work, from holiday, from hospital, from events and occasions happy and sad. Ultimately, we all return home after our deaths - to God, to the heavenly homeland, perhaps to the depths of the great ocean of divine love, compassion and embrace where, in the words of the blind Church of Scotland minister and hymn writer George Matheson, our own lives may have a richer and fuller flow.

Perhaps, as some have suggested to me when I have discussed this theme with them, we would do better to use the Celtic term 'peregrination' today rather than pilgrimage with its connotations of destinations, churches and cathedrals, relics, shrines and holy places. Following the Celtic way of *peregrinatio* means going out of our comfort zones, being prepared to go to places and experience situations which may make us uneasy and uncomfortable, taking the risk of wasting time, getting lost, letting go and not being in control. That is what will make us people on and of the Way, followers of the Son of Man who has nowhere to lay his head.

I ended my previous books on Celtic Christianity with a poem, not necessarily of Celtic provenance. For *The Celtic Way* I chose 'You who would travel the highway of faith' by Mervyn Wilson, for *Colonies of Heaven* 'Some people travel in straight lines' by Julie McGuinness, and for *Columba: Pilgrim and Penitent* John Bell's 'From Erin's shores, Columba came'. After much deliberation I have decided to end this book with a poem which, even although it is presented here in an English translation, is in its original form of relatively early Celtic origin. It is one of those attributed to Columba. Pilgrimage is very clearly its central and abiding subject. It weaves together several of the themes found in Celtic Christianity – the connection between the inward journey of faith and the outward physical *peregrinatio*, the rhythm of setting out and returning, the sense of being surrounded by the hosts of heaven of as well as of being supported by the stout earth, the concept of life and faith as a path which Christ both shows us and shares with

us. In these and in other respects it captures something of what is
involved in following the Celtic way.

The path I walk, Christ walks it.
May the land in which I am be without sorrow.
May the Trinity protect me whenever I stray,
Father, Son and Holy Spirit.
Bright Angels walk with me - dear presence - in every dealing.
In every dealing I pray them that no one's poison may reach me.
The ninefold people of heaven of holy cloud,
The tenth force of the stout earth.
Favourable company, they come with me,
So that the Lord may not be angry with me.
May I arrive at every place, may I return home;
May the way in which I spend be a way without loss.
May every path before me be smooth,
Man, woman and child welcome me.
A truly good journey!
Well does the fair Lord show us a course, a path.

Bibliography

A.M. Allchin, *Praise Above All: Discovering the Welsh Tradition* (University of Wales Press, Cardiff, 1991)

A.M. Allchin, *God's Presence Makes the World* (Darton, Longman and Todd, 1997)

Bede, *The Ecclesiastical History of the English People* (Oxford World's Classics, 1999)

Ian Bradley, *The Celtic Way* (Darton, Longman and Todd, 1993)

Ian Bradley, *Columba: Pilgrim and Penitent* (Wild Goose Publications, Glasgow, 1996)

Ian Bradley, *Celtic Christianity: Making Myths and Dreaming Dreams* (Edinburgh University Press, 1999)

Ian Bradley, *Colonies of Heaven* (Darton, Longman and Todd, 2000)

Ian Bradley, *Believing in Britain* (I.B.Tauris, 2007)

Brendan Bradshaw, 'The Wild and Woolly West: Early Irish Christianity and Latin Orthodoxy' in *Studies in Church History* 25 (Ecclesiastical History Society, 1989)

Sheila Cassidy, *Sharing the Darkness* (Darton, Longman and Todd, 2002)

Thomas Clancy and Gilbert Márkus, *Iona: The Earliest Poetry of a Celtic Monastery* (Edinburgh University Press, 1995)

Tim Clarkson, *Columba* (John Donald, Edinburgh, 2012)

Hugh Connolly, *The Irish Penitentials* (Four Courts Press, Dublin, 1995)

Caitlin Corning, *The Celtic and Roman Traditions: Conflict and Consensus in the Early Medieval Church* (Palgrave Macmillan, 2006)

Oliver Davies, *Celtic Christianity in Early Medieval Wales* (University of Wales Press, Cardiff, 1996)

Oliver Davies, ed., *Celtic Spirituality* (Paulist Press, New York, 1999)

Oliver Davies & Fiona Bowie, *Celtic Christian Spirituality* (SPCK, 1995)

Wendy Davies, 'The Myth of the Celtic Church' in Nancy Edwards & Alan Lane, eds., *The Early Church in Wales and the West* (Oxbow Books, Oxford, 1992)

G.R.Evans, *A History of Pastoral Care* (Cassell, 2000)

T.Gilby, ed., *St Thomas Aquinas Theological Texts* (Oxford University Press, 1955)

Louis Gougaud, *Christianity in Celtic Lands* (Four Courts Press, Dublin, 1992)

Miranda Green, ed., *The Celtic World* (Routledge, 1996)

Kenneth Jackson, *Studies in Early Celtic Nature Poetry* (Llanerch Publishers, Felinfach, 1995)

Michael Lapidge, ed., *Columbanus: Studies on the Latin Writings* (Boydell Press,1997)

Richard Loomis & Dafydd Johnston, *Medieval Welsh Poems* (Binghamton, New York, 1992)

James Mackey, *An Introduction to Celtic Christianity* (T & T Clark, Edinburgh, 1989)

John Macquarrie, *Paths in Spirituality* (SCM Press, 1972)

Gilbert Márkus, 'The End of Celtic Christianity', *Epworth Review*, Vol.24, No.3 (July 1997)

Donald Meek, 'Celtic Christianity: What is it and when was it?', *Scottish Bulletin of Evangelical Theology* 9, No.1 (1991), pp.13-21.

Donald Meek, *The Quest for Celtic Christianity* (Handsel Press, Edinburgh, 2000)

Gerard Murphy, *Early Irish Lyrics* (Clarendon Press, Oxford, 1965)

Diarmuid O'Laoghaire, 'Soul-Friendship' in Lavinia Byrne (ed.), *Traditions of Spiritual Guidance* (Geoffrey Chapman,1990)

Thomas O'Loughlin, *Journeys on the Edges: The Celtic Tradition* (Darton, Longman and Todd, 2000)

Thomas O'Loughlin, *Celtic Theology* (Continuum, 2000)

John J. O'Meara, *Eriugena* (Clarendon Press, Oxford, 1988)

Eugene Peterson, *The Message* (NavPress, Carol Stream, Illinois, 1993)

Charles Plummer (ed.), *Vitae Sanctorum Hiberniae*, Vols I & II (Four Courts Press, Dublin, 1997)

Oliver Rackham, *Transitus Beati Fursei* (Fursey Pilgrims, Norwich, 2007)

Andy Raine & John Skinner, *Celtic Daily Prayer: A Northumbrian Office* (Marshall Pickering, 1994)

B.R.Rees, *The Letters of Pelagius and His Followers* (Boydell Press, 1991)

B.R. Rees, *Pelagius: A Reluctant Heretic* (Boydell Press, 1988)

Hilary Richardson, 'The Concept of the High Cross' in Michaeal Ritter, ed., *Irland und Europa* (Kiett-Cotta, Stuttgart, 1984)

John Ryan, *Irish Monasticism* (Four Courts Press, Dublin, 1992)

Edward Sellner, *Wisdom of the Celtic Saints* (Ave Maria Press, Notre Dame, 1993)

Richard Sharpe, ed., *Adomnan of Iona: Life of St Columba* (Penguin Books, 1995

Robert Van de Weyer, *Celtic Fire* (Darton, Longman and Todd, 1990)

Bibliography

G.S.M.Walker, *Sancti Columbani Opera* (Dublin: Dublin Institute for Advanced Studies, 1957)